Desi Disruptors

Praise for *Desi Disruptors*

'*Desi Disruptors* is a masterclass in Indian brand-building. With razor-sharp insights and gripping storytelling, it reveals how some of the most iconic brands didn't just find markets—they created them. A must-read for every founder, marketer and business leader looking to build a brand with enduring consumer love.'

—Kunal Bahl,
co-founder, Snapdeal and Titan Capital

'This is a highly enjoyable book that presents the journey of some iconic Indian consumer-facing brands. Each story is packed with information and insight. Meticulously researched, this book is a great read and should inspire more and more Indian entrepreneurs to become desi disruptors.'

—Ambi Parameswaran,
independent brand coach, advertising veteran, bestselling author

'*Desi Disruptors* is a powerful tribute to the brands that dared to dream differently. As someone who believes in clean innovation and deep consumer insight, I found this book to be both inspiring and immensely relevant to India's evolving entrepreneurial story.'

—P.C. Musthafa,
founder, iD Fresh Food

Desi Disruptors

TIMELESS LESSONS FROM ICONIC INDIAN BRANDS

VISPY DOCTOR
AND
VIKRANT PANDE

HARPER
NON-FICTION

First published in India by Harper Non-Fiction 2026
An imprint of HarperCollins *Publishers*
HarperCollins *Publishers* India, Cyber City,
Building 10-A, Gurugram, Haryana – 122002, India
www.harpercollins.co.in

2 4 6 8 10 9 7 5 3 1

P-ISBN: 978-93-7307-915-8
E-ISBN: 978-93-7307-427-6

NON FICTION/BUSINESS

Typeset in 11/14.2 Minion Pro
by HarperCollins *Publishers* India Pvt. Ltd

Printed and bound at
Repro India Limited

FSC
www.fsc.org
MIX
Paper from responsible sources
FSC® C047271

This book is produced from independently certified FSC® paper to ensure responsible forest management.

HarperCollins Publishers, Macken House, 39/40 Mayor Street Upper,
Dublin 1, D01 C9W8, Ireland

For my wife, Villy, and son, Ashdin—both rockstars in their own right. So proud of them!

—Vispy Doctor

Contents

Preface

'Insight is a consumer truth which has not been worked on,' says Vispy, distilling a profound concept into a single sentence. But what lies beneath this statement is a relentless quest—a journey into the human psyche that drives the most successful brands to rise above the rest.

Santosh Desai, the razor-sharp CEO of Futurebrands, frames it differently, yet succinctly: 'It is the unexpected vision of the obvious.' This hauntingly elegant phrase defines the brilliance of insight—a moment of clarity in a fog of assumptions. Vispy, a veteran of countless focus groups, knows this well. His mastery lies in coaxing unspoken truths from consumers—truths that are felt but never articulated until the right moment, the right question and the right listener unlock them.

But not everyone believes in the power of questions. Market-research legend Paco Underhill dismisses them entirely. To him, the truth isn't told—it's revealed through silent observation, where the nuances of human behaviour betray deeper realities.

Subhash Kamath, adman and storyteller, builds on this thought: 'There are so many types of differentiation—product, communication, distribution—but the marketer's true pursuit is uncovering that untapped need, the one the consumer feels but hasn't voiced.' And so, marketers navigate these shadowy terrains, hunting for insights that bridge the gap between consumer desires and the products or services waiting to serve them.

One story stands out—a chilling yet ingenious innovation. In the UK, a surge in attacks on women highlighted a horrifying truth: When threatened, fear often silences victims, robbing them of their voices. The solution? A whistle designed to pierce the air when screams cannot, its shrill frequency both disorienting attackers and summoning help. From there, other products emerged—doorstop alarms for hotel rooms and portable safeguards that promised women peace of mind. Such innovations don't just fill a gap, they reshape markets and redefine how brands connect with the deeper fears and needs of their consumers.

Throughout this book, you'll encounter stories like this, where you, with the benefit of hindsight, may think the solution to be obvious, rather than ingenious. But why didn't others act on the same insight? The answer lies in the rare alchemy of intuition and execution. Marketers who achieve greatness are those who listen to their instincts but temper them with a disciplined understanding of consumer behaviour. David Ogilvy says (or at least the line is attributed to him) that people don't think what they feel, don't say what they think and don't do what they say. Insights, thus, are derived from observation and not direct questioning.

Paco Underhill famously remarked, 'The obvious isn't always the apparent.' This sentiment separates mere observations from insights. Observations, like data points, are static—facts waiting for meaning. Insights, however, dig beneath the surface to uncover the 'why' and the 'how'. They turn the mundane into the transformative, unlocking paths to action that elevate brands into leaders.

Take the example of Coke's iconic 'Thanda Matlab Coca-Cola' campaign. At first glance, it seems simple—almost too obvious. 'Thanda' (cold) was a colloquial synonym for cold drinks. But Coke went deeper, recognizing a cultural gap: Cold drinks were seen as urban, elitist and disconnected from rural India. The insight wasn't just about language, it was about bridging two worlds. With Aamir Khan embodying a spectrum of rural and urban characters, Coke didn't just sell a drink—it redefined what it meant to be cool: Rooted in Indian reality, yet aspirational.

Other marketers, too, have turned simple truths into seismic shifts. Kishore Biyani's Big Bazaar didn't mimic global giants like Walmart. Instead, he embraced India's love for chaos and crowds, creating a mela-like atmosphere in his stores. Shoppers weren't intimidated; they felt at home. The cluttered audio of announcements, music and chatter wasn't a flaw—it was a feature, echoing the vibrancy of Indian markets. Biyani didn't just sell products, he sold an experience—a uniquely Indian blend of tradition and modernity.

The brilliance of consumer insights often lies in their emotional depth. Agnello Dias, the creative force behind countless campaigns, explains the distinction: Product insights highlight gaps—price, convenience, occasion—while communication insights tap into unspoken emotions. 'Parents loving their children' is a tired trope. But portraying a husband who instinctively walks on the traffic-facing side to shield his wife? That's a fresh, relatable insight. It's these subtle truths, mined from human behaviour, that make brands unforgettable.

Consider the legacy of Dove's 'Real Beauty' campaign. The insight wasn't groundbreaking—beauty comes in all shapes, sizes and colours. But the execution—a celebration of diversity—touched a nerve in an industry that had long excluded many. Similarly, Nike's controversial campaign with Colin Kaepernick showed the power of taking a stand. While divisive, it resonated with a core audience, reinforcing Nike's identity as a brand unafraid to challenge norms.

Closer to home, campaigns like Tanishq's ad on remarriage or Surf Excel's 'Daag Acche Hain' series didn't just sell jewellery or detergent—they redefined societal narratives. Tanishq celebrated second chances and evolving family structures, while Surf Excel turned messy clothes into symbols of love, exploration and learning.

These stories share a common thread: the courage to go beyond the obvious. Insights, as Darshan Patel, the founder of Paras Pharma, demonstrated, aren't born in boardrooms or spreadsheets. (He launched some of India's most successful brands like Livon, Krack Cream, Set Wet Gel, Fogg, and many others) They emerge from life itself—rooted in human behaviour and brought to life through relentless execution. Patel's iconic brands weren't mere products; they were solutions to unarticulated needs, guided by intuition and bolstered by action.

As Martin Lindstrom, author of *Buyology: Truth and Lies About Why We Buy*, points out: 'The better we understand how consumers think, the better we become at predicting the future. And the only way we can truly understand how consumers think is by ignoring what they say.'

This is the paradox of insights: The consumers may not know—or say—what they truly want. Henry Ford famously quipped, 'If I had asked people what they wanted, they would have said faster horses.' The visionary marketer doesn't just listen; they anticipate, interpret and create.

The pages that follow are filled with such visionaries—brands that defied convention, marketers who trusted their gut but grounded it in strategy, and insights that turned the ordinary into the extraordinary. They teach us that leadership isn't about playing it safe—it's about daring to see what others overlook and having the audacity to act on it.

Compiling the list of brands for this book was not easy, especially with our focus on actionable consumer insights. India boasts a vast landscape of brand leaders across countless categories, making our initial selection daunting. To narrow it down, we adhered to two crucial criteria.

First, we needed direct access—a conversation with the promoter, advertising guru, brand head or CEO. We wanted to hear the story straight from the 'horse's mouth'. Second, the brand's journey had to reveal a powerful core consumer insight. Without these two elements, many deserving brand leaders, despite our keen interest, were not included.

It's vital to state up front: This list is far from exhaustive. We've undoubtedly missed many phenomenal Indian brands and their inspiring journeys, which we eagerly anticipate covering in future editions. We genuinely welcome your suggestions for leaders we should feature next!

You'll notice some internationally recognized names like Vicks, Whisper, Maggi, Jockey and Volvo in these pages. While not Indian by origin, their inclusion is deliberate. Their stories offer a unique window into how multinational powerhouses masterfully uncovered and leveraged uniquely Indian consumer insights to achieve market leadership here. It's a fascinating study in localized success.

Not every brand profiled here is a reigning champion. Some, like Coldarin, may no longer dominate, but their compelling narratives offer valuable lessons. Others, like Puro, are carving out niche success against formidable competitors, proving that impact isn't always about scale. Weikfield offers a truly unique journey, while Itch Guard and Ring Guard showcase brilliant examples of identifying and filling market gaps. And the story of Taj Hotels is a masterclass in building a world-class experience through meticulous consumer research and feedback. We included these brands, and others mentioned in the book, because their stories offer unique insights.

Vispy and his dedicated team at Ormax Consultants have shaped countless brands over four decades. While their expertise is invaluable, some insights remained proprietary, preventing their inclusion.

We've meticulously crafted these brand stories through extensive interviews. While every effort has been made to ensure accuracy, minor factual discrepancies in figures, revenue shares or timelines might have inadvertently slipped in during individual narrations. Additionally, because many narrations discuss events that happened years ago, it's possible the narrator may not remember the sequence of events or facts correctly. We encourage you to notify us if you spot any. More importantly, we urge you to immerse yourself in and learn from these profound insights.

Another point we would like to highlight is this: Many readers will have observed that most of the brands launched by Darshan Patel were aggressively promoted through television ads. The promoter believed in the value of advertising and did not dismiss it as a wasteful expenditure. He spent money on television, especially during the Doordarshan era. This showed his faith in media investments. While we do not elaborate on his philosophy of bombarding the consumer with advertisements, we thought this was an important point to note. Relentless communication of the core idea has helped Darshan Patel's brands remain leaders.

Ultimately, we hope these brand journeys ignite a spark, inspiring you to create the next generation of desi disruptors!

PART ONE

How to Create a Blue Ocean

A senior executive from one of India's largest conglomerates once proclaimed, 'We don't fight for market share; we create markets!' This bold declaration encapsulates the essence of visionary branding—where success isn't about competing for existing customers but about redefining the landscape itself. We'll explore how iconic brands carved out their own markets, effectively rendering the competition irrelevant and, in doing so, established themselves as industry leaders.

The brands we studied didn't merely settle for capturing a slice of the market share, they set out to create entirely new markets. For consumers, alternatives are always available—local brands, home remedies, even makeshift solutions. But the revolutionary brand sees an opening in this chaos, a gap to not just enter but transform the marketplace, building something fresh and enduring. As brand guru Santosh Desai aptly puts it, 'If a brand can connect its core idea to the subconscious of people and position itself as the solution to their needs, it creates a market of its own to dominate.'

Brands that broke through did so by identifying and addressing unfulfilled consumer needs. They researched habits, preferences and desires previously overlooked by others. By tapping into this gap, they didn't just build a business—they established leadership. Sometimes, the catalyst is a simple innovation—a new technology or a reframing of an existing product—that propels a brand to the top, making it the default choice for consumers. A prime example is the rise of Frooti, which, thanks to a game-changing technological breakthrough, secured its place as the number-one choice for decades. More on that later.

Consider the example of sanitary napkins, where the challenge wasn't merely to compete with other brands but to shift an entire cultural mindset. It wasn't about beating competitors head-on—it was about addressing a deeper issue: changing entrenched social habits. As the CEO of a cola giant once famously remarked, 'The competition for colas isn't other brands, it's water.' Similarly, Whisper's rise to dominance wasn't just about competing with other brands, it was about redefining social attitudes and empowering women. Though Whisper is part of the multinational Procter & Gamble, its story is deeply rooted in addressing uniquely Indian challenges. Changing social norms takes time and, in India, it demands patience—a patience that has been amply rewarded with Whisper's continued leadership in the market.

The journey of Colgate further exemplifies this slow yet steady transformation. For decades, Colgate has worked tirelessly to change consumer habits in India—from the use of the traditional datun (chewing stick) and local herbal powders to the gradual adoption of toothpaste. This wasn't a campaign for quick wins—it was a long-term strategy, one that spanned decades and continues to this day. Colgate's leadership in oral care wasn't won overnight—it's a result of several years of consistent effort and an unwavering commitment to changing deeply ingrained consumer behaviours.

At the heart of many of these powerful brands lies an emotional connection. Worldwide, a mother is the symbol of compassion, care and love—a universal figure that transcends cultures. This mother figure plays a pivotal role in branding, and many successful brands have leveraged this symbolism to forge an immediate bond with their consumers.

Vispy, founder of Ormax Consultants, constantly seeks insights into consumer behaviour, often through travel or focus groups. In one of their studies, they uncovered the secret behind Vicks's unparalleled success in India. Vicks didn't sell just another cold remedy—it sold the comfort of a mother's touch. Vicks didn't attempt to convince consumers that it was a cure for the common cold (because, as we know, there is no actual cure). Instead, it focused on the emotional appeal of soothing comfort, subtly positioning itself as a product that provided relief in the form of a mother's loving care.

Despite being a multinational brand, Vicks became deeply ingrained in the Indian household, emerging as a product that was not only trusted but also revered. What made Vicks unique in India was its formulation—it remained a balm, unlike in other countries, where it shifted to syrups and tablets. This decision reflected an acute understanding of the Indian market, where consumers weren't looking for just a remedy, but the comforting touch of familiarity. Vicks's genius lay in communicating that the product wasn't about medication—it was about soothing and comforting care. And in doing so, it became a brand that is not just a product but a trusted companion in the battle against the common cold.

Let's now delve deeper into the story of Vicks and its incredible journey to becoming the undisputed leader in its category.

1

VICKS: 132 YEARS YOUNG

Bharat Patel, the then CEO of Richardson Hindustan, which launched Vicks in India, tells us the story of how the product was invented:

> Vicks has helped relieve cold and cough symptoms for over 132 years. The journey began in 1894, when a young pharmacist named Lunsford Richardson opened a store in Greensboro, North Carolina, to address the needs of his community. Lunsford created remedies to treat the ailments of his family, friends and neighbours, becoming a trusted member of the community for the care he provided. He quickly developed a family of twenty-one remedies and began to sell them under the Vicks name. The most popular of these remedies was the Croup and Pneumonia Salve, which Lunsford created to soothe his own young son's severe cough. The boy soon recovered. Today, we know this product as VapoRub.
>
> Lunsford chose 'Vicks' over his own name as he was an avid gardener and saw an advertisement for 'Vick's Seeds'.

> He felt it was short, easy to remember and looked good on a label. Dr Joshua Vick was also the name of Lunsford's brother-in-law and, as the long-serving town doctor, he was equally trusted in the community and was happy to allow Lunsford to use his last name for his line of products. Years later, the very boy who inspired the salve would change its name to Vicks VapoRub and sell it in the familiar blue jar.

Bharat Patel throws in a little bit of trivia before we get down to the business of understanding the challenges faced in India while launching the brand. 'In German-speaking countries (apart from Switzerland), it is sold under the name "Wick VapoRub" to avoid a branding blunder, as "Vicks" when pronounced in German would sound similar to a vulgar word.'

He adds another bit of information. 'The novel ingredient in Vicks was menthol, or mint camphor, then being imported as a "wonder drug" from Japan. No one had yet thought of putting it in cigarettes. But that is a story for some other day,' he guffaws.

'We asked many chemists which was the most popular remedy for cold and the answer was Vicks VapoRub. It is, by far, a leader, according to them. While we were not challenging market statistics, the product was clearly the pharmacists' choice,' he adds.

Vicks faced multiple challenges when it launched in India. Chuckles Dr P.M. Bhide, a general physician, 'Till today, despite advancement in medicines, there is no clear cure or medicine for the common cold. Ironical, isn't it?' And this was only one problem of many that Vicks faced. It was selling a remedy for cold, without actually saying it in so many words.

'How was the company to market a product not as a cure for [a] cold but [as] something which soothes and makes the child feel relief, while giving the mother fewer sleepless nights?' asks Bharat Patel. 'Since we launched Vicks in India, we have continued to dominate the market and be the default choice for the customer.' A sprightly man in his late seventies, Bharat Patel still recalls his days with Richardson Hindustan Limited before it was acquired by Procter & Gamble (P&G) in 1985. We were lucky to meet Bharat Patel in his Vadodara home, which he visits once in a while when not globetrotting.

Adds Sonali Dhawan, a senior executive at P&G, based in Dubai, in relation to another problem Vicks had to tackle: 'Unlike other products of P&G, Vicks is in the healthcare space. One doesn't use such products on a daily basis. So the entire communication and market research required a different approach.'

The owner of a pharmacy who didn't wish to be named says, 'The blue jar of Vicks VapoRub is a ubiquitous restorative for [the] common cold in homes in India, and it evokes not only nostalgia but there is a sense of familiarity as well. It has been around since the 1960s, if I remember correctly.'

He is not far off the mark. What we are here to understand is how did the company tackle the problems it faced. Not only was there no cure for a cold but it was not a product which would be used unless someone suffered from the common cold. How would the brand become so familiar that the consumer would reach for nothing but Vicks when suffering from cold?

Bharat Patel tells us that Vicks was introduced in India in 1964—six decades ago! He talks of how they did an extensive study of the market to educate the customer and understand what she wanted. Gurcharan Das, the ex-CEO of P&G (he was Bharat Patel's boss), talks of how Vicks reinvented itself as the 'one offering relief for common cold'. Das had joined the company just a couple of years after Vicks was introduced in India. During one of his visits to Surat, he found a housewife adding a spoonful of Vicks to boiling water. She then asked Das to inhale the vapours emanating from the mixture. Das had found a new use for Vicks!

Elaborates Bharat Patel on another problem that Vicks faced in the market, 'There was a strong negative association with Vicks in the eastern markets. They believed that Vicks would choke the lungs and arteries as it contained camphor. Our main market was in west and south India. We were able to penetrate many markets by showcasing the idea of Vicks in hot boiling water; but it still was around 15 per cent of the total sales, not more. Nevertheless, it helped highlight another way of using Vicks.'

For a brand to become successful, it has to be widely available across retail formats. A challenge Vicks faced was that it was categorized as an 'allopathic medicine' and thus was allowed to be sold only in pharmacies. This needed to change. If Vicks wanted to be available everywhere, including retail stores, it had to shed its 'medicine' tag. The change, however, happened due to circumstances the company had never envisaged—a pharmacy strike across the nation!

It was Bharat Patel who came up with the idea of rebranding and repositioning Vicks as an Ayurvedic product. 'We convinced the concerned regulatory agencies that Vicks contained Ayurvedic ingredients, thus qualifying it as an Ayurvedic product. This was done as we were facing a nationwide strike by pharma shops, who were demanding a higher margin. And so, out of sheer necessity, we created this unique positioning. As an Ayurvedic product, Vicks could be sold as an OTC [over-the-counter] product and be made available in every kirana shop! Thanks to the strike, we had turned a problem—that of being restricted to pharmacy stores—into an opportunity!'

'Long-lasting, fast-acting performance is what a customer looks for in a product,' Bharat Patel says with regard to how a customer sees a product for cold and cough.

His thoughts on market research echo what we believe, and have heard from many marketing and advertising gurus:

> You do research when you have a choice. I ask my brand managers whether the research is nice to know or whether we really need it. I believe that 'nice to know' research is a waste. We launched [Vicks] as an Ayurvedic product to prevent regulatory hurdles but, for the customer, it was something

> which had been prescribed by the doctor. The customer needed a product which was endorsed by the doctors.
>
> The Ayurvedic tag allowed us to go from 75,000 shops to 8 lakh shops instantly. Those days, we used to call cosmetic shops 'bangle stores' as they used to sell bangles. Vicks started selling in these shops too.

The keen insight gleaned from what Bharat Patel trashes as 'regular and nice to know research' was the whole element of a 'loving touch', which only a mother could provide. The child, when she is suffering from a bad cold, needs a touch that soothes.

Explains Bharat Patel how Vicks was all about a mother's love, talking of the famous ads which showed a mother rubbing Vicks on her child's chest:

> We sell mother's love for Vicks and ageless beauty for Oil of Olay. We are in the business of selling emotions.
>
> We had captured the mother–child combination which no one else could. All pharma companies tried to copy Vicks. Glaxo[SmithKline], Pfizer, Warner, Johnson [& Johnson], Ranbaxy ... all of them tried but couldn't sustain. Because we were not selling a product alone. We had understood what appeals to the customers. Remember the ad where the young boy, played by actor Jugal Hansraj, comes home drenched and the mother shouts at him for having exposed himself to the rain? He then gives her a bunch of flowers which he had picked up for her. When he says, "Happy birthday, Mummy!" the mother chokes with emotion.
>
> Symptom, Action, Relief: That was our formula. Even the sneeze in our ads was real; it would, at times, take fifty takes, but we would get it right,' says Bharat Patel with a chuckle as he recalls the shoots.

Vicks faced another challenge while launching its cough drops, a brand extension for sore and itchy throats, a regular symptom for someone suffering from the common cold. The company researched on what would appeal to the customer. Merely showing the product as providing relief for a cough was not enough. It had to be something which appealed to the problem the customer faced. 'The communication had to touch the right chord—the vocal chords, in his case,' says Bharat Patel with a laugh, while explaining the methodology used.

It is Harish Shivdasani from IIM Ahmedabad, whom Bharat Patel credits for the research on Vicks cough drops. 'It was the first time that such research was done. Harish found that the customer perceived the cough drops at three different levels. At a conscious level, it was a merely a remedy for a sore throat. At an unconscious level, it was adult candy; and at the subconscious level, it provided oral gratification. This insight of oral gratification is what sold the product. And it was a blockbuster!'

He tells us how the ad was conceived. 'Vicks ki goli lo, khich khich dur karo' is a tagline familiar to anyone who watched television in the late 1980s and 1990s. The seeds of the commercial were sown in Japan.

'Aur phir bhediye ne memne se kaha ki "main tumhe khaa jaaonga"'—in this, a father is telling the story to his daughter, which is cut short as he is seen clearing his throat. And a spiky little bug is seen banging against the walls of his throat. Next, he consumes a triangle-shaped tablet which makes the bug disappear. The Japanese campaign had referred to the bug as the "Ahemm bug", as it was named in the US and other countries.'

'I was the head of marketing at Richardson Hindustan, and I discussed this ad with Piyush Pandey of Ogilvy,' he says. 'We realized that we couldn't call it the "Ahemm bug". And everyone zoomed in on calling it "khich khich". The jingle "Gale mein khich khich, gale mein khich, kya karoon? Vicks ki goli lo, khich khich dur karo" was written by Pandit Vinod Sharma. We used Harish Bhimani's voice for the father.'

When the company decided to launch a 'cold remedy' in the form of a tablet, it faced a challenge as there were existing brands in the market which promised the same cure for the same symptoms. It was a product extension as a remedy for adults. Vicks VapoRub, with the loving mother's touch, was a blockbuster, and the company felt there was a need to target the 'adult' market next. But before launching the product, there was a need to research the gap and positioning. There was a gap in the market but to position the product, clear research was needed.

A brand extension needs to be clearly thought through, lest it is seen merely as an 'adult' version of what is essentially a children's product. This was the challenge P&G faced. Brand extensions are tricky, and we have seen many companies fail when tempted to extend the brand to a different segment.

Brand extension is a strategy that involves leveraging an established brand name to launch new products in different categories or markets. This approach capitalizes on the brand's existing recognition and customer loyalty to increase the likelihood of success for the new offering. However, it carries several risks, such as brand dilution, mismatch with consumer expectations, cannibalization of the existing brand and potential market rejection, especially if the extension significantly deviates from the brand's core identity.

There are notable examples of failed brand extensions by global multinationals, which, in hindsight, raise questions about the initial decision to expand into those categories. In 1982, Colgate, a brand synonymous with toothpaste and oral care, ventured into frozen meals. Consumers struggled to associate the Colgate name with food, resulting in the product's failure. Similarly, in 1989, Pepsi introduced Pepsi AM, a coffee-flavoured soda aimed at the breakfast market. The concept faltered because it failed to align with consumers' expectations of soda as a refreshing beverage, particularly in the morning.

There are innumerable examples of such failures—much more than successes. To ensure success, it is crucial that there is consistency with brand values. The new brand or product should align with the core values and image of the original brand. Consumers need to recognize the extension as a natural fit, not a departure from what they trust.

The story of how Vicks Action 500 was launched shows the unique approach P&G used to discover a gap in the market. It was a brand extension with a thought-through strategy and backed by extensive research.

Consumer research showed that people from the south and west of India preferred balms like Amrutanjan, while north Indians liked quick solutions for their colds. This was the insight the marketing team gleaned.

Elaborates Bharat Patel, 'We are the General Motors of cough and cold—we had to do something about it.' He chuckles as he adds, 'Ironically, we found that later the southern states became our best markets!'

There was a reason P&G named the brand Vicks Action 500. Bharat Patel explains:

> Those days, there was Aspro and Aspirin for cold and cough, but their dosage was 250 mg each, which was suitable for children. Adults needed to take two tablets. We launched a caplet [tablet in the shape of a capsule] as an OTC product, while with other brands one needed a prescription for consumers to buy them. We made our caplet a single-dose product versus the double doses prescribed by other brands. And unlike the white colour of the other prescribed medicines, we kept the caplet colour yellow. We called it Vicks Action 500. The word 'action' was to signify jumping back into action and the number 500 was selected for rural folks to remember easily.

Aspro and Aspirin focused on headaches, which normally accompanies the common cold. There was a gap in the market for a single solution to colds, headaches and stuffy noses, and the brand that came up with this could potentially occupy a leadership position.

Those who remember the ad will recall how the character is troubled with a bad cold and is about to take a pill for his headache when the voiceover asks, 'Sardi se pareshaan, sar phat raha hai aur naak bhi band?' When the character nods in frustration and snaps, 'Haan, bhai, haan', the voiceover once again asks, 'Toh phir sar dard ki goli kyun?'

Says Bharat Patel:

> Other brands like Saridon with their jingle 'Saridon … sar dard se aaram' were focusing on headaches. Here comes Vicks Action 500, a medicine for headache, cold and a choked nose, all rolled into one. It hit home the message that this is the medicine to go for. And it worked. We soon had a 50 per cent market share.

The marketing team created further momentum by telling the customer that Vicks Action 500 would be a remedy for all his problems. And it worked!

The product was a runaway success. Bharat Patel shares his favourite anecdote in this regard:

> In the mid-1980s, an advertisement carried in *Nai Dunia* created a lot of excitement in Bhopal. The ad for Vicks Action 500 asked readers to tear out an accompanying coupon and exchange it at the nearest drugstore for two free tablets. People redeemed the offer in hordes, with one drugstore owner collecting some 30,000 coupons! P&G officials suspected foul play and further investigations revealed that the enterprising man had ordered a reprint of 15,000 copies of *Nai Dunia* and cut out the coupons. His logic: The newspaper cost him 50 paise and the two tablets were priced at ₹1, and he also got an extra 10 per cent as handling charge. Unfortunately, he didn't make a penny! But it showed us the power of our brand.

Even today, the caplet enjoys a 50 per cent market share in the cold tablet category and is clearly the leader.[1]

In the US and many other countries, for P&G, the market has moved to variants of Vicks in the form of syrups and tablets like NyQuil and DayQuil. In India, however, the idea bombed. P&G experimented with Vicks Action 500 Night, a cold tablet to be taken at night, and it didn't work.

Nevertheless, Vicks, and its extensions like Vicks Inhaler, continue to be winners in the P&G stable—it has straddled the leader board in India for half a century now as India's number-one healthcare brand.[2] And it will continue to do so.

The success of Vicks and its brand extensions clearly tells us that if the right consumer sentiment is tapped, the brand will continue to occupy the leadership position. It makes a space for itself, leaving the competition far behind. With Vicks VapoRub, it clearly leaned into the idea of providing a 'mother's loving touch' and has continued to be the brand a mother reaches for when her child is suffering from a cold. Likewise, by realizing that the consumer was looking for a tablet which solved multiple symptoms, Vicks Action 500 grabbed the position in the customer's mind and continues to remain the preferred choice.

Vicks showed how a brand can 'create a market'. To create a blue ocean, the brand has to go where none has ventured so far. And if there is a proposition which appeals to the consumer, which connects to the emotions of the user, it will swim in that ocean as a brand leader.

---

1. Vinod Mahanta, 'Vicks Action 500: The pill that cheers', *The Economic Times*, 25 February 2004, https://economictimes.indiatimes.com/vicks-action-500-the-pill-that-cheers/articleshow/517237.cms?from=mdr, accessed on 1 April 2025.

2. *2022–23 Annual Report*, Procter & Gamble Hygiene & Health Care Limited, https://in.pg.com/2023_annual_report.pdf, accessed on 1 April 2025.

Mother's love has always been the heart and soul of Vicks, and it continues to work its magic, transcending time. When hunger strikes, it is once again the mother who becomes the ultimate saviour, the one the children turn to. And if a brand can tap into the very core of a mother's conscience—stirring a sense of responsibility so powerful that it makes her feel both the weight of feeding her children and the immense pride of offering them something healthy, hearty and, most importantly, quick—it has struck gold.

Does this sound familiar? It should. This is the tale of Maggi, where the art of nurturing and the promise of convenience merge to create a legacy.

Along the roadside in Panchgani, we were having lunch at a restaurant run by one of the many 'Maggipreneurs' thriving in the country, when we discovered the success formula of Maggi. Vispy is a foodie, and while slurping on noodles and soup, we talked of Maggi. Ormax has done many focus groups for a variety of food products. Vispy says:

> It is not easy to enter a food business and become a generic name in its category. Food habits are the hardest to change. Trust me. We have helped launch more than a dozen food products—be it masalas, pickles, papad or salt—and it has been a challenge each time. Changing food habits is challenging because they are deeply ingrained in cultural, emotional and routine behaviours, making consumers resistant to adopting new products. Successful marketing must overcome this inertia by emphasizing on convenience, taste or health benefits to drive gradual acceptance.

Nestlé faced this problem of launching a food product which was known to most Indians but was not popular enough to be in the kitchen on a daily basis. To make a food product successful it had to become a staple part of the diet or at least a very popular product which is demanded almost daily. The food brand had to enter the household—and stay put!

This is where Nestlé's Maggi makes for an interesting study.

2

MAGGI: THE TWO-MINUTE REVOLUTION

Nestlé faced many challenges when it launched Maggi Noodles. But a deep understanding of consumer insights, backed by solid research, made the brand a blockbuster in every sense. 'If "Xerox" is synonymous with photocopiers and "Colgate" means toothpaste, then "Maggi" stands for instant noodles,' quips Subhash Kamath, an advertising veteran. Someone else once said that 'Google is for search, while Maggi is for instant noodles.'

A history buff and a Maggi fan overhears our conversation and joins in. 'Did you know the story of Maggi begins in the scenic town of Kemptthal, Switzerland, in the late nineteenth century?' he asks us. 'It was here in 1884 that Julius Maggi, a young and enterprising entrepreneur, set out to revolutionize the way people cooked. Recognizing the growing need for quick and nutritious meals, he developed the formula for a concentrated, flavour-packed soup mix that could be prepared in minutes. This innovative product laid the foundation for what would later become the Maggi brand. His goal was to provide a practical solution for busy families who lacked the time to cook wholesome meals at home. Recognizing the increasing number of women entering the workforce, which would leave them with less time for traditional cooking, Julius Maggi saw a genuine demand for affordable, delectable meals that could be prepared swiftly and effortlessly.' We are impressed with the young Maggi fan's knowledge and thank him for it.

We note that while Maggi was launched in 1884, it would take another century before it would be seen in India. While Maggi has become a generic name for noodles today, it didn't become a phenomenon overnight. Once again, we see tremendous research and insights when a brand wants to enter into the food space.

It was the early 1980s. Nestlé had ventured into the food space with Maggi Magic Cubes but had not met with much success there. It was natural for any marketer to launch a product after analysing and segmenting the market, identifying met and unmet needs. New products have a chance to succeed only if they find a way to fulfil the consumer's needs, whether articulated or not. The discussion in the Nestlé India management team was about launching noodles.

The management felt that if Nestlé Malaysia could sell noodles in tons, why shouldn't the same success be seen here in India? The question was: Does the customer always know what she needs?

Food business is tricky and establishing new food habits are not easy. Kellogg's struggled for years to 'change the breakfast habit of Indians', offering cereals meant to be eaten with cold milk, while most Indians preferred a hot breakfast, like idlis, parathas, upma, poha, and so on.

Establishing credibility in the food industry can be difficult, especially with a new brand. Consumers need to trust that the product is safe, delicious and high quality. Luckily, Nestlé scored well on these parameters as it was a company which was trusted for its high-quality and safe baby products like Cerelac.

How was Nestlé going to succeed in India with noodles? When launching a food product, consumer insights are invaluable to ensure the product resonates with the target audience, and addresses their needs, preferences and pain points. The Nestlé India management was keen—having seen tremendous success in other countries—to launch Maggi in India. But the problem they faced was that in India, in the early 1980s, noodles were regarded as 'Chinese food' and were consumed occasionally, when one went to a restaurant. Kolkata was the only exception where, thanks to the large ethnic Chinese population which had settled there decades ago, noodles were commonly consumed. Food habits don't change overnight. 'Mexican or Mediterranean food even today is not mainstream,' says a food blogger.

The key challenge for Nestlé India was figuring out which culinary product could provide the right breakthrough in India.

Preliminary research showed that there were no industrially produced food products sold in large quantities in the 1980s, and most of what customers ate was homemade, using fresh ingredients. The question then was: Would instant noodles ever become part of the Indian food repertoire? Nestlé studied the market to understand what Indians ate from breakfast till dinner, and how noodles could become a part of a regular meal. The problem statement, while simple, was perplexing: What should Nestlé do to make noodles a daily consumption habit?

Quite naturally, it needed out-of-the-box thinking, backed by research which uncovered insights. The product had to be presented not merely as noodles but as something far bigger and more encompassing. Nestlé wanted to ensure that it had got the fundamentals answered, like what did the noodles stand for, what problem was it solving and how did the consumer decode the benefits. There were questions raised, like would the consumer eat noodles? Does it substitute breakfast or a different meal? What were the noodles competing against and at what price points?

Quite naturally, all this meant deeply understanding food habits across all regions. India has a wide variety of cuisines—if the Chennai customer has idlis for breakfast, the customer in Punjab was gorging on parathas with pickles or curd.

Initial research showed that, across India, no matter what state or region, the housewife spent a lot of time preparing meals, as food was considered serious business. Lunch was not eaten together as the husband was in office, while the children were at school. Many children had lunch after returning home from school. The other insight was that homemade snacks took a long time to make, whether pakoras or pav bhaji. As with the Indian palate, most dishes were served hot. A cold dish was considered lazy and didn't suit the palate of most consumers. For instance, cold sandwiches were not very popular as a snack.

In a situation where changing food habits is not easy, how was Nestlé going to launch its noodles? The research showed a way out. There was an opportunity to try the snack market, as the housewife was willing to experiment there with children. Mothers were willing to take liberties. In the case of kids, hunger pangs needed to be satiated fast. There was an opportunity to provide a 'quick-cooking snack', research showed. Pepsi and Haldiram's had not launched their potato chips yet, and even if some local chips were available, mothers were hesitant to provide them as an alternative as they were not home-made and were not considered healthy. Secondly, she was not adding any value to the meal. Simply tearing open a pack and serving it to the kids would seem lazy and inappropriate for a mother. To come to the right conclusion, further research was needed, and Nestlé decided to conduct detailed qualitative primary research, in-depth interviews and group discussions with mothers and kids to understand what they were thinking. The research showed their reactions to the concept and what was the most appealing way to insert the brand into the market.

Sangeeta Talwar, then a newly minted management graduate, describes the process in great detail in her book *The Two-Minute Revolution.*[1]

---

1. Sangeeta Talwar, *The Two-Minute Revolution: The Art of Growing Businesses* (Gurgaon: Penguin Random House India, 2018).

After many studies, it was decided that Maggi Noodles would best fit the role of a hot and fresh snack—especially for kids returning home from school, as it was not seen as unhealthy.

But most products, unlike today, were not bought by children as they were not the decision-makers. Today, however, a lot of kids are taking these decisions—thanks to social media and shopping websites. But in the 1980s, the decision-maker was the mother. The product had to appeal to her. This is where the right communication needed to be researched in great depth—and where Nestlé came out was a winner and has been one for past many decades.

The problem statement for the communication team was to steer Maggi Noodles away from being seen as traditional noodles and appeal to the average middle-class Indian mother. Maggi Noodles had a chance to occupy a hitherto vacant position as an instant snack that was seen as healthy and one which the mother liked to prepare.

As we have seen in Vicks and other advertisements, appealing to the 'mother's love' has always worked in India. The proposition for Maggi was to showcase the noodles as something that was quick to cook, and which could be served hot and with mother's love—all to satiate the hungry child. The idea was to have the mother or the housewife's involvement in the 'preparation' of the snack so that she could eliminate the guilt of offering something 'ready-made'.

It was meant to be a snack for kids. While, eventually, Maggi went on to become a snack or meal for all age groups, that was not the case when it was launched. 'The communications team came up with the idea of a "fun element" showing 'long strands of slippery noodles that wound and unwound themselves around the fork and the kids dangling a strand and allowing it to hang out of their mouths as they slurped up their bowl of fun', says Sangeeta Talwar.[2]

The guilt that a mother might feel for serving a meal straight out of a packet was obliterated with a masterstroke of brilliance. The solution? A vibrant explosion of vegetables, added with care as

---

2. Sangeeta Talwar, *The Two-Minute Revolution*, pp. 2–13, 38 and 39.

the noodles cooked, transforming a simple, ready-made dish into a feast of freshness. This clever move didn't just make the meal more enjoyable, it turned the narrative on its head, elevating the noodles from the realm of 'unhealthy' to a dish bursting with nutritional value. What was once a source of concern became a triumph, a testament to the power of a mother's love and ingenuity.

After finalizing the target audience, Nestlé worked on Maggi's advertisements. The advertising agency Hindustan Thompson Associates (now J. Walter Thompson or JWT) was asked to create the commercial, which was eventually made by Prahlad Kakkar. The words '2-minute' were specifically used in the TV commercial instead of 'instant'. 'Two minutes' was easy to understand in any language, and it also emphasized its convenience and how it saved time. We see a child saying, 'Mummy, bhook lagi hai!', to which the mummy says, 'Bas do minute.' This not only acted as a huge trigger among children and their mothers but it also catapulted the brand into a cultural movement. Maggi tapped extensively into emotional storytelling to showcase indulgent moments in a mother–child dynamic and propagated the idea of free-spirited youngsters, representing modern India. Maggi's '2-minute' video ads on TV showed consumers how to cook the noodles. 'Consumers saw that there were only two to three steps in cooking, and that those steps were very simple, familiar and easy to implement. It didn't demand any special skills. This was an important element of success in communicating something simple and easy to cook and serve,' says an advertising executive who worked on the Maggi brand at the time of its launch

The focus Sangeeta Talwar gave Maggi is worth noting. This is what makes a brand stand out and remain a leader for decades. In the initial years, the research team and the advertising agency would go out every few months to see the response. They found that, for the first few years, adults were eating as much Maggi as young children, but Nestlé didn't shift its focus and continued to engage with children. Says Talwar in her book, 'Along with a growing target pool of consumers who would be indulged by their parents, as pockets grew warmer, getting a larger share of the wallet would not be that difficult. As these kids grew, they would perhaps carry their love for Maggi with them into adulthood.'[3]

This kind of strategy needs long-term thinking. If a brand has to remain a leader for decades, it needs to think decades ahead and not get carried away by short-term gains or losses.

Maggi has evolved beyond a mere household snack into a thriving enterprise, giving rise to 'Maggipreneurs' who innovate with the product to sustain their livelihoods. As of 2022, Maggi continues to hold nearly 60 per cent of the noodles market in India.[4] (An industry insider, who didn't want to be quoted, estimates the noodles market to be around ₹12,000 crore.) Be it a local chai wallah or a food-stall vendor, at street corners or on highways, Maggi is often listed as a hot food they can serve. Even on hikes and adventure camps, a pack of Maggi Noodles is a trusted companion for travellers. It has become a familiar taste and a recognizable aroma that is adored by Indians. Eaten anytime, anywhere, it requires very little to cook a hot, quick and tasty snack.

Maggi's success lay in making people buy the product frequently. It involved enticing users to develop a craving for the taste of the noodles. In other words, the brand manufactured a new habit among users. Once a habit was formed, the user was automatically triggered to buy the product and use it. There was no need for any external prompt.

After a phenomenal run since its launch, Nestlé faced its biggest test in 2015, when Maggi was suddenly banned in India.

---

3. Sangeeta Talwar, *The Two-Minute Revolution*, pp. 2–13 and 131.
4. Aaren Panikar, Sana Sidhu, Noor Fatima Moolji and Varsha Agarwal, 'Maggi out of a "big soup"', *International Journal of Advance Research, Ideas and Innovations in Technology*, Vol. 8, Issue 5, https://www.ijariit.com/manuscripts/v8i5/V8I5-1202.pdf, accessed on 4 April 2025.

It is always interesting to see how a leader brand reacts when embroiled in a controversy. This is where a deep understanding of the consumer helps to not only help a brand recover but come back stronger from where it was before the controversy erupted.

Let us look at a few examples before we dive back into the Maggi story. These examples will help us understand how global leaders managed different crises and helped the brand win back its glory.

Readers may be aware of the famous Tylenol controversy and how Johnson & Johnson (J&J), the brand owner, reacted. It is a classic case of crisis management.

A little background about the case: In 1982, seven people in Chicago died after consuming Tylenol capsules laced with cyanide. The tampering occurred after the product had left the production line, but it created a massive public health scare and severely damaged consumer trust in the brand.

J&J took immediate steps to recall 31 million bottles of Tylenol, costing the company over $100 million. But the prioritizing of consumer safety over financial loss really resonated with the public. The company also introduced innovative safety measures like tamper-proof packaging, including foil seals and childproof caps, to prevent future incidents. J&J focused on rebuilding trust by launching a marketing campaign emphasizing its commitment to safety and quality, and offering incentives such as discounts and free replacements to encourage consumers to try their products again. J&J adhered to its core value of putting customers' safety and well-being first, earning public trust.

Within a year of the crisis, Tylenol regained much of its market share. The company's proactive, transparent and customer-focused approach turned a potential brand-ending catastrophe into a case study in effective crisis management. Tylenol not only recovered but also strengthened its reputation as a trustworthy brand.

Let us look at another example where a global giant like Coca-Cola made a strategic error in interpreting market research and how it successfully navigated the crisis, emerging stronger than before.

The story of New Coke is one of the most famous examples of turning a corporate misstep into a marketing triumph. Coca-Cola launched New Coke in April 1985, changing its original formula for the first time in nearly a century. The decision was based on research suggesting that consumers preferred the sweeter taste of New Coke in blind taste tests, as compared to Pepsi and the original Coke. Loyal Coca-Cola consumers were outraged, seeing the change as an attack on an American icon. Negative feedback poured in through protests, media criticism and over 40,000 angry calls and letters to Coca-Cola. The backlash grew into a cultural phenomenon, with many demanding the return of the original formula. Realizing its mistake, on 11 July 1985, just seventy-nine days after launching New Coke, Coca-Cola announced the return of the original formula under the name Coca-Cola Classic. This move was framed as a response to overwhelming customer demand, emphasizing that the company 'listened to the people'.

The media frenzy around the New Coke debacle created an unprecedented level of attention for Coca-Cola, but by admitting their 'mistake' and bringing back Coca-Cola Classic, the company portrayed itself as a brand that valued and respected its loyal customers. Coca-Cola did not immediately discontinue New Coke; instead, it was marketed alongside Coca-Cola Classic for several years as an alternative for those who preferred its taste. This allowed the company to appeal to different customer segments without alienating traditionalists. The reintroduction of Coca-Cola Classic resulted in a sharp rise in sales. By the end of 1985, Coca-Cola's market share had significantly increased, surpassing Pepsi. Consumers who had taken Coca-Cola for granted now rallied behind the brand, reinforcing their emotional connection to the product.

The story of New Coke became a part of American pop culture, and is still studied as a case of brand loyalty and marketing genius. Coca-Cola demonstrated the power of listening to customers and owning mistakes; the controversy and subsequent resolution strengthened Coca-Cola's brand identity. By changing the original formula, Coca-Cola had unintentionally made people realize how much they valued it, creating an emotional rallying point. The decision to bring it back in the form of Coca-Cola Classic was executed in a way that made the brand seem responsive and consumer-focused. Coca-Cola used the extensive media coverage of the controversy to keep its brand in the spotlight and reframe the narrative.

The New Coke episode is now considered one of the most effective examples of crisis management and brand reinforcement, proving that even a perceived failure can become a winning strategy with the right response.

Coming back to the Maggi story, Nestlé had never imagined that it would face a crisis threatening the very existence of Maggi Noodles. But problems don't come with a warning! How Nestlé reacted is a case study in regaining brand repute and trust.

A little background: Business was growing at a tremendous speed till 2015, when a major controversy threatened to disrupt the entire business for Nestlé. Maggi was banned for six months across India after the Lucknow Food Safety and Drug Administration found much-higher-than-permissible amounts of lead and MSG (monosodium glutamate) in samples of Maggi's 2-Minute Noodles. Maggi had an impressive 80 per cent market share,[5] which dropped to zero when the controversy erupted. Nestlé needed to take swift action apart from following up in courts. In a few months, the court had ruled in favour of Nestlé, and the company was ready to relaunch the product.

This is where smart management came in. Customers had trusted Maggi for decades, and it was important to win that trust back. Merely launching the product alone was not enough. Nestlé had been receiving a lot of messages from customers who overwhelmingly loved Maggi. Plus, there was anger, as many felt cheated by the findings of

5. Sounak Mitra, 'The Maggi ban: How India's favourite two-minute noodles lost 80% market share', *Livemint*, 16 February 2017, https://www.livemint.com/Companies/1JKHsutTXLWtTcVwdIDg0H/The-MAGGI-ban-How-Indias-favourite-twominute-noodles-lost.html, accessed on 1 April 2025.

the food safety authority. While research showed that the customer inherently trusted Nestlé as a company which would not cheat them, they still needed assurance. Nestlé had built up huge brand equity from 1983 to 2015, and they could not afford to let this wither away.

The management understood that it was important to engage with the customer directly. The 'We Miss You Too' campaign' was thus launched, which seemingly mirrored the customer's feelings, seeing as Nestlé had received thousands of messages. It helped that influencers like Ram Gopal Varma, the acclaimed film-maker, went on social media praising Maggi too. Once the court case was won, it was crucial to win back the trust of the mother—the primary customer who felt vindicated that she had not been giving unsafe food to her children. After all, she had trusted Maggi for years and she couldn't be wrong.

Nestlé decided against a national launch and chose instead to operate on the e-commerce platform Snapdeal. The deal went viral with 60,000 packs sold in five minutes! Normal distribution soon followed, with Maggi's advertisements reiterating the fact that the people were waiting for it. Hashtags such as #DILKIDEALWITHMAGGI started trending on Twitter after the sale resumed. After receiving an overwhelming response to the flash sale, Maggi conducted various online competitions asking consumers to express their favourite moments and feelings about Maggi's comeback. Consumers participated with full enthusiasm. The brand's Twitter, Facebook and YouTube pages were filled with fans expressing their trust in Maggi. The company thus set the stage for Maggi's official comeback in India. In no time, it regained a market share of 57 per cent by the third quarter of 2016, reclaiming a major chunk of its lost glory.[6]

---

6. 'Maggi Noodles reclaims top spot with 57% market share', *Brand Equity, The Economic Times*, 23 August 2016, https://brandequity.economictimes.indiatimes.com/news/business-of-brands/MAGGI-noodles-reclaims-top-spot-with-57-market-share/53821448, accessed on 1 April 2025.

There were suggestions to change the brand name as the 'Maggi' brand had been sullied, but better sense prevailed. After all, the brand enjoyed salience, loyalty and trust built over decades, and the company not only stuck to it but later added variations of the product, thus increasing its market share. In January 2018, to mark thirty-five years of Maggi in India, Nestlé launched a new marketing campaign aimed at negating all the fears about the safety of the product. The campaign contained two promotional videos. The first, a proposed television campaign titled 'Kuch Achha Pak Raha Hai' focused on the changing status of women. The other featured the complete manufacturing process of Maggi Noodles, which showed consumers the eight stages of making Maggi, from the farm to packaging in retail form.

'We had already built the connect with the customer,' proudly recalls Emmanuel Upputuru, who was with the ad agency Publicis when Nestlé celebrated twenty-five years of Maggi. 'The customer, who was a child two decades ago, had a lot of stories to tell as he or she had grown up. Some were parents now.' Nestlé launched the 'Me and Meri Maggi' campaign with Publicis, where customers were asked to send in their personal Maggi stories. To Nestlé's surprise, they received around 30,000 stories. The anecdotes about Maggi were humorous, touching and sincere, whether it was related to hostel life, camping outdoors, impressing the girlfriend or being served Maggi during the 2005 Mumbai floods or the tsunami tragedy of 2004. The selected customers were then featured in ads and on packets of Maggi. The soldier, the cook, the bride and every mother had a story to tell. The three best stories were recreated as films. 'Sales were rocketing,' says Emmanuel.

'Two minutes had turned into twenty-five years of joy. When people own the brand, magic—or shall I say "Maggi"—happens!' Emmanuel says cheekily as he laughs out loud.

There are many learnings from Maggi's initial launch. The brand becoming synonymous with noodles in India is testimony to its scale of success. It has created a market for noodles when nothing of that sort existed in the country. Maggi caught customers when they were young. Instead of targeting the adult population, Nestlé sold Maggi as a snack for children, who were much more open to trying new foods. But it strategically made the mother the partner. Nestlé continued to focus on children knowing that they would become the largest brand ambassadors as they grow. Nestlé realized the value of India's largest demographic. Through extensive research, the company understood the pain points of a mother. Nestlé recognized that working women and homemakers alike always struggled to make evening or after-school snacks for kids that were both filling and tasty. Nestlé sold Maggi as that snack. The product attribute was clearly defined. Since this was a mid-meal snack, the preparation had to be quick and simple! Nestlé was aware of the guilt a mother would feel while preparing a ready-made snack. Maggi was an instant meal but Nestlé, by showing vegetables in its preparation, made the mother feel like she was preparing a healthy snack and relieved her of the guilt.

Any other brand would have either been destroyed or its position taken forever by a competitor had it suffered the kind of negative publicity that Maggi got when it was banned in 2015. As we saw earlier, the Nestlé management's proactive approach worked to ensure Maggi was revived. The Maggi ban highlighted the importance of building and maintaining trust, credibility and transparency with consumers and stakeholders. Maggi used emotional campaigns like 'We Miss You Too' and 'Nothing like Maggi' to reach out to customers.

Trust once gained, and then regained, is the biggest source of strength for a brand. And Maggi continues to be the leader as one of the most trusted brands in India. The country has emerged as the world's largest market for Nestlé's Maggi, with a whopping 6 billion servings sold in the financial year 2023–24, Nestlé's annual report states.[7]

If trust is an important criterion for success in the food industry, it becomes even more crucial when it comes to personal hygiene products like sanitary napkins. We will see that in our next story.

---

7. *2023–24 Annual Report*, Nestlé India Limited, https://www.nestle.in/sites/g/files/pydnoa451/files/2024-06/Annual-Report-2023-24.pdf, accessed on 1 April 2025.

3

WHISPER: BREAKING A TABOO

Vispy and I found ourselves journeying into the heart of a slum near Bandra, part of an NGO initiative that would soon reveal uncomfortable truths. Vispy, deep into research for a new product aimed at improving sanitation, knew this slum was the perfect setting for his focus groups. But it was the conversations that followed—about something so fundamental, yet so often overlooked—that would haunt us.

A woman, who runs an NGO and chose to remain anonymous, told us, 'Less than 20 per cent of women and girls in rural India—and even in slums like this one in Mumbai—use sanitary napkins.' Her words cut through the air, heavy with the weight of an issue most of us take for granted. We weren't stunned—no, we had heard the statistics before—but we were undeniably shaken.

Vispy, with the sharp insight of someone who has spent years immersed in market research, added grimly, 'When you measure market potential by per capita consumption, or rather, the shocking lack of it, the sanitary-napkin market is nearly at the top of the list for untapped opportunities.' The silence that followed spoke volumes.

What we had witnessed was not just a market gap—it was a glaring social crisis.

Even today, in India, consumer awareness is lacking. This was the opportunity Procter & Gamble (P&G) saw when they created Whisper, which occupies a pride of place in the brand portfolio. 'Adoption of sanitary napkins is less than 20 per cent in India, whereas adoption of cosmetics like lipstick is significantly higher at 65 per cent,' says Chetna Soni, VP at P&G India.[1]

The challenge Whisper faced was on multiple fronts. There were already brands of sanitary napkins in the market, but the larger population needed education. There was a clear lack of understanding of the product, not to mention very poor usage even in places where knowledge resided. It was a challenge Whisper decided to tackle head-on, but with a lot of long-term thinking and patience. They were clearly looking decades ahead and fighting to win the war, not the battle.

The story of Whisper is not just interesting but educative.

While researching for sanitary-napkin brand Whisper, we ask Sangeeta* (who runs an NGO dealing with menstrual education in the slums of Mumbai) about the history of sanitary pads.

> Menstrual pads have been mentioned in history as early as the tenth century in ancient Greece, where a woman is said to

*Name changed on request

1. Karuna Sharma, 'Adoption of sanitary napkins is less than 20% in India, whereas adoption of cosmetics like lipstick is significantly higher at 65%: Chetna Soni, P&G', *Business Insider*, 26 April 2021, https://www.businessinsider.in/advertising/brands/article/adoption-of-sanitary-napkins-is-less-than-20-in-india-whereas-adoption-of-cosmetics-like-lipstick-is-significantly-higher-at-65-chetna-soni-pg/articleshow/82219127.cms, accessed on 2 April 2025.

> have thrown one of her used menstrual rags at an admirer in an attempt to get rid of him.
>
> Before the disposable pad was invented, most women used rags, cotton or sheep's wool in their underwear to stem the flow of menstrual blood. Knitted pads and rabbit fur, even grass, were all used by women to handle their periods.
>
> The very first disposable pads were thought up of by nurses looking for new methods to stop excessive bleeding, particularly on the battlefield. The first pads were made from wood-pulp bandages by nurses in France. It was very absorbent, and cheap enough to throw away afterwards. It was Johnson & Johnson in America that developed its own version in 1896 called 'Lister's Towel: Sanitary Towel's for Ladies'. The problem was women did not feel comfortable asking for this product.

We nod in agreement as the problem still continues in many parts of India, especially rural India and within the urban poor. But Sangeeta talks of a much larger problem, that of menstrual hygiene and management.

This is where the Whisper story becomes more relevant. We speak to Rohini Miglani, vice-president, brand-building integrated communications at P&G, who has been with the company since the launch of brand Whisper. She tells us:

> When P&G launched Whisper in India in 1989, there was a very large, untapped market, and a strong competitor in Johnson and Johnson which had the Stayfree and Carefree brands. The initial brand strategy was against those brands, which were belted, bulky and not very comfortable. Whisper thus decided to focus on competition conversion initially. But it soon realized there was a larger segment to tap rather than focus on competitors.

To create a blue ocean—a market where competition is irrelevant and untapped potential thrives—a brand must differentiate itself through bold and innovative action. Instead of merely carving out a small slice of the existing market, Whisper chose to redefine the landscape entirely. The true challenge in much of India was the widespread lack of sanitary-napkin usage, despite the vast number of potential customers. Recognizing this gap, Whisper saw limitless opportunity. If even a fraction of this underserved majority were to embrace the product, the brand would experience unparalleled success.

This is where a bold move from P&G received not just visibility but brand recall and sales as well. Consumer research showed that speaking about periods and sanitary napkins openly was a taboo subject—to the extent that Doordarshan, the state TV broadcaster, and the only TV channel available then, didn't allow ads for sanitary napkins till 11 p.m., and even those were heavily censored. Rohini and team were convinced that if they wanted buyer behaviour to change, they had to not only be bold but also direct while talking to the customer, the woman in this case, and show her the problems she faced.

The P&G team met the then information and broadcasting minister to convince him why the ads were relevant as the company was trying to educate women about using sanitary napkins, which had a massive hygiene factor attached to it.

Earlier, the ads were all indirect—talking of 'those days', and showing girls on cycles with white pants and how they were 'carefree', thus endorsing the Carefree brand.

Whisper launched a 'bold' ad starring Renuka Shahane. When it was taboo to talk of periods, here was a popular face speaking openly about her discomfort. In the advertisement, a young Renuka stares at the viewer and starts by saying she has something to tell everyone. The ad is almost like a confessional. She says that she uses Whisper which doesn't allow her wetness to feel uncomfortable and that she is able to sit for hours without discomfort. She goes on to say, 'Whisper is so dry that I have forgotten wetness.' The ad ends with the line:

'Whisper—such cleaner, drier protection that you'll forget what wetness feels like.'

The ad was a big hit and sales started moving upwards. More importantly, Whisper was suddenly seen as a brand that spoke the language of women. Technology changes helped, and the new advanced product, using gel, which was used in P&G's diapers as well, led to a significant change, as the size of the sanitary pad was reduced considerably.

Says Sonali Dhawan, a senior P&G executive based in Dubai:

> We started off with having a difficult time getting permissions to advertise on prime-time television and then we partnered with Renuka Shahane, the star of the long-running TV series *Surabhi*, where she narrated her experience of having found a solution to make her periods much more comfortable. This was 1993. That's how Whisper became the first brand to show a sanitary pad in a commercial, the first to mention the word 'periods' in advertising and the first brand to show how the product works in an advertisement.

Consumer research showed that sanitary pads were still mostly used in urban areas and that there was a very large untapped market. This is where some FMCG companies had made a mark, making shampoos and detergent in affordable, small-sized sachets.[2]

Adds Rohini Miglani, 'I was deeply involved in the process of educating girls in schools, a campaign which has been running now for nearly twenty years. It is internally called KGIS—Keeping Girls in School.'

---

2. Chinnikrishnan of CavinKare, which produces Chik shampoo, is a legendary figure today, thanks to his revolution of selling shampoo in a sachet.

Sonali explains, 'Cloth conversion is a long-drawn process. A cloth sanitary napkin, which is reusable, costs less than ₹20, while Whisper pads were three times the price.'

Rohini and team did a lot of market and consumer research to understand the problem. 'This is where storytelling has played a role,' she tells us. She describes her experience which is captured in the book *Lead with a Story* by Paul Smith.[3]

In 1993, Rohini Miglani was the new brand manager for Whisper feminine pads in India. She was conducting in-home research with consumers in Chennai. Rohini says that she had just fifteen names and addresses of middle- and lower-income women who had agreed to be interviewed, and that she was hoping to understand what had compelled them to recently depart from using simple cloth pads during their menstrual period and instead spend significantly more on Whisper. It has been decades but Rohini can still recall vividly the day that changed everything.

'The day was a disaster as most of the addresses were either wrong or the concerned people were not at home. I couldn't understand Tamil and that was a big challenge. I was desperate for a meaningful dialogue with at least one customer. Chennai was hot, humid and dusty.'

Rohini tells us about her first interaction with a real customer:

> I entered a home to find the fan not working. The woman smiled apologetically and gestured me to sit on one of the two metal folding-chairs by the front door. I collapsed gratefully onto it. As I slowly sipped from the metal tumbler of water she gave me, I took in my surroundings. It was a poor man's house with two rooms and a small kitchen. A tattered curtain tried to conceal the kitchen. The room was decorated with a jar of plastic flowers kept at the window, while the usual garish

3. Paul Smith, *Lead with a Story: A Guide to Crafting Business Narratives that Captivate, Convince, and Inspire* (New York: Amacom, 2012).

> calendar was seen hanging on the wall. And on the table under the window, neatly kept, were a pile of school exercise books, primly covered in the regulation brown paper.

Rohini says that it became clear to her that there was a serious schoolgoing child in the house. She adds, 'I felt bad that I was interviewing a housewife, tired from the day's work and what was probably her siesta time before the child returned from school.'

Rohini asked the woman whether she used Whisper but she shook her head, saying it was for daughter, who was in class eight, and who was earlier using cloth. Rohini asked why she had started spending money on Whisper when she could use cloth too.

'It's because she has to go to school, you see,' the woman replied.

Rohini was there to understand the real reason for them moving from cloth to Whisper and she persisted. The mother finally answered, 'We could use cloth, but she was not comfortable and couldn't concentrate on her studies. Now, she doesn't have to worry about stains and any wet feeling.'

Rohini asked her, 'Don't you think Whisper is expensive?'

She tells us, 'I was surprised at her answer as she said yes, it is expensive but her daughter needed it to be able to concentrate in school and get good marks. She continued as she knew my next question and said she wanted her daughter to study and not get married soon.' Rohini probed a little, asking what was wrong in getting married early. 'I was shocked when the mother leaned forward, looked into my eyes, her tiredness gone. She said she didn't want her daughter to become like her and that she wanted her to be financially independent.'

'I was taken aback at her intensity,' Rohini admits. 'Her last line was what hit the nail on the head. She said, "I don't have many aspirations of my own but I want my daughter to be different and that is where Whisper makes sense to me!"'

It was an aha moment for a researcher like Rohini—that Whisper was making a difference to someone's life to such an extent. That a mother could aspire to see her daughter not missing classes and being on her way to the financial freedom which comes with education.

When Rohini and her research team returned to office, they wrote a proper clinical summary of their own conclusions and observations. It contained all the expected details, describing the consumers they met as an amalgam of the dozen women interviews during the week. The most effective vehicle she left for helping others understand the consumer was the intimate portrait contained in her personal meeting with one woman. It's been circulating for almost two decades now and helps new Whisper employees understand their consumer to this day.

The biggest challenge, as Sangeeta from the NGO mentioned, was about menstrual hygiene. Most girls were using cloth and this led to a lot of problems. It was something P&G decided to tackle head-on. The challenge was manifold—that of education and then converting the prospect to a potential buyer of a sanitary napkin, which was many times the cost of a simple cloth.

Rohini explains how Whisper systematically addressed the problem of cloth conversion. As mentioned earlier, the brand realized that not only was the subject of menstrual cycles a taboo, Indian textbooks mostly didn't have a chapter on menstruation and, whenever it was taught in schools, the teachers tended to skip the chapter altogether. It was something no one wanted to talk about openly, despite being such an important issue. Rohini elaborates:

> The success of Whisper was a combination of product breakthrough and the school programme. This is where the KGIS programme, running for more than twenty years, has made a difference. P&G found that Indian textbooks don't have a chapter on menstruation and that boys don't know about it at all. And even when taught, it is only to girls in school. It is estimated that nearly 23 million girls drop out of school every year due to this reason.

The campaign 'Missing Chapter' by P&G (created by Leo Burnett) has been a tremendous success and is the most awarded advertising campaign in Indian history. The ad shows a girls' school where the girls are seen passing a red piece of paper to each other. When caught in the morning assembly, one of the girls is asked to read the note in front of everyone. She begins: 'Periods!' And then goes on to explain how periods are natural, they happen to every girl and that it is not a disease; rather, it helps her become a strong woman. When the principal says she could be suspended for this, the girl replies that millions of girls are missing this chapter in their lives. The entire school assembly applauds and the principal smiles.

Rohini tells us:

> The red paper in the ad became a powerful symbol of a period revolution in India, appearing everywhere in the media. The campaign was validated when, in a historic decision, the Government of India agreed to include the missing chapter on periods in public school books. Smriti Irani, minister of women and child development from 2019 to 2024, who used to be a model many years ago, recently tweeted about periods too, thus continuing the effort to destigmatize the issue.
>
> With a view to further break the taboo around periods and the superstitions associated with it, we came out with our award-winning campaign 'Touch the Pickle'. There is a common perception in many parts of India that if a woman who is on her period touches a pickle jar, the pickle would get spoilt. We focused on challenging the myths around periods and sparked a nationwide conversation around these archaic practices. This campaign also earned India its first Grand Prix in the inaugural Glass Lions at the 2015 Cannes Lions. Around 30 lakh people directly participated in the campaign and we earned around 1200 million impressions across different media.

The P&G ads talked about 'woh paanch din' and spoke about periods openly. The ads depicted blood as red, instead of using blue ink which other companies used to show the absorption quality of the pads. Such direct communication is a double-edged sword. While most other players were hesitant to show blood, P&G took the bold step of going all out and this helped it earn the trust of consumers who felt connected with the product.

Rohini used extensive consumer research to understand how to tackle the problem. The first insight was that in the sanitary-napkin market the competition talked about absorption without showing blood directly. White pants and such were meant to show how the sanitary napkin absorbed well. The entire communication was about protection, freedom and such benefits. Research showed that while customers talked about protection, the deeply felt need was that of 'dryness', which was not explicitly mentioned. This is where smart insight helped uncover the unspoken need.

Market research showed that the competition didn't address the customer directly but spoke about experiences. P&G decided to not shy away from the real issue in their advertisements. This appealed to women, who felt as if Whisper understood them.

Rohini says:

> Another insight about school education led to the KGIS programme. It started with sampling. We knew we had a great product with the technology we had from the US. We used sampling as a route to create awareness. In our massive sampling programme, we used both free and discounted napkins. But the agenda is reaching out to schools. It is a below-the-radar programme where we don't talk of it but actually *do* at the ground level.

Another insight was about teaching the sales promoters of the napkins what to say. This was the genesis of the KGIS programme. While sampling, the promoter talked about why napkins helped children remain in school, and that there was no fear of dropping out and missing classes.

Yet another insight gleaned from market research was about many customers talking about the 'heavy-flow days'. The research team found that there was a significant correlation between girls who had a higher BMI and a heavier flow. The ad agency then decided to use models who were not conventionally slim, but those who represented what the research was showing. The models spoke about 'those heavy-flow days' and how Whisper helped. Rohini explains:

> We had a lot of competition, especially from cloth. We were now talking of converting from cloth, which we couldn't compete with on price. It had to be something different. We found through research that cloth protection was good but limiting due to its bulkiness; it was uncomfortable, and the girl couldn't run and have fun. Also, the chances of leakage were very high.

The insight was 'not feeling wet' as against 'just talking about dryness'; Rohini says it was a genius move in copy writing. Whisper ads were making a difference as they articulated the unspoken need of the customer, who felt that Whisper understood her problems. Great market research is about uncovering the unspoken need—and Whisper had done precisely that.

Insights are useful, provided the marketer knows how to use them. The genius of a marketer lies in being able to ignore customer feedback, provided there is a genuine belief in the product and communication strategy. Various pieces of research had shown that P&G's direct approach, talking about periods, meant that boys were seeing the ads and were likely to ask questions that would make the parents uncomfortable. P&G ignored the feedback, as they were convinced that periods were just a bodily function, and that knowledge and education were crucial. More importantly, the competition was avoiding talking directly with the consumer, which was a differentiator for Whisper. The courage to ignore customer feedback is something rarely seen. Insights need to be used properly. Insights are about what is unspoken and not necessarily articulated. What is articulated, as in this case, would have been counter-productive to Whisper's long-term agenda.

The Whisper product had to ensure that technology played a key role. Customer habits in India are very different. On days when the woman uses a napkin, she uses one napkin for the entire day, while in the Western world, the woman changes twice a day and, in some countries, like Japan, she changes every few hours. Sonali says, 'The P&G technology has helped to not only make the napkin thin and lightweight but also provide total protection, and not allow the "feeling of wetness".'

Adds Smiti Jain, brand director, P&G:

> We continuously do research to understand our customer and her voice. For example, the woman, say, ten or twelve years back, was scared, timid, afraid of talking about her periods. Today, she is more open. Earlier, her equation with her mother or father was not as candid as it is today. The girl of today doesn't allow her periods to dictate her life. We built that in our communication. Earlier, the girl was just a prop, a recipient. Now, she is the change agent, in form of an elder sister or a friend who is recommending Whisper.

Another insight the Whisper team discovered was with regard to how women perceived nights. They were worse than the days as, during the day, at least she had control over leakage, in the night, she was sleeping uncomfortably, worried that she may stain the bedsheet. There was a feeling of helplessness. This was an opportunity to launch a range of products that lasted longer. 'These products earlier had a 3–4 per cent share, while, today, they contribute nearly 15 per cent of our sanitary-pads business,' Smiti says.

The sanitary-napkin market is huge, and growing. As per the IMARC Group, a leading market research company, the Indian sanitary-napkin market reached US$825.3 million in 2024. Looking forward, the research shows the market is expected to reach US$1,227.1 million by 2028, exhibiting a growth rate (CAGR) of 9.5 per cent between 2023–2028.[4]

'There is tremendous competition,' Smiti admits. 'But we tackle the same with technology and innovation. Whisper Ultra is a case in point, where the product, while priced high, is unbeatable. We showed in our bold ad how when the pad is squeezed, not a drop comes out. The "no-wet feeling" came about from market research, and it has helped business tremendously.'

She continues, 'Today, with 120 million users of Whisper and a business of US$320 million, almost ₹2500 crore, the brand is a huge one for P&G.' And the brand continues to grow, maintaining its leadership position with a substantial 51 per cent market share.[5]

There are many learnings from Whisper for any brand trying to create a blue ocean market for itself. It didn't take a piece of the market share but created a market for itself. Going against the grain is a bold strategy, but if there is a technologically superior product, an understanding of the consumer mindset, a willingness to confront reality and plenty of patience, there is lot to gain in the long term. This is what the Whisper story tells us.

4. IMARC, 'Indian Sanitary Napkin Market Report by Product Type (Disposable Menstrual Pads, Cloth Menstrual Pads, Biodegradable Menstrual Pads), Distribution Channel (Supermarkets and Hypermarkets, Pharmacies, Convenience Stores, Online, Specialty Stores, and Others), and Region 2025–2033', https://www.imarcgroup.com/indian-sanitary-napkin-market, accessed on 2 April 2025.

5. Nisha Qureshi, 'Whisper's take on the competitive menstrual hygiene market in India', AFAQS, 11 December 2024, https://www.afaqs.com/marketing/whispers-take-on-the-competitive-menstrual-hygiene-market-in-india-8426075, accessed on 2 April 2025.

Whisper is a great example of how a brand created a market for itself by not going after small and irrelevant competitors, compared to the potential market size, but tried going back to the basics of understanding customer behaviour and creating awareness to break the taboo around periods. P&G's marketing team was able to glean insights from research by creating ads which were counterintuitive but appealed to their consumers. The women felt Whisper understood their problems well. Whisper spoke their language.

Creating a market requires patience. Most brands look for short-term gains. The school programme of Whisper is a classic example of long-term brand building and has reaped dividends for P&G. The brand is a great listener as is seen in its ads about 'heavy-flow days', and ads which showed 'real women' and not the typical skinny models which many brands used. Building a brand means training even the sales team to speak the language appropriate to the target segment. And when it is educative in nature, talking to schoolgirls and their parents, it needs a different approach.

With such insights, Whisper is clearly India's leading feminine hygiene brand[6] and will continue to remain so. It is a success story with many learnings.

---

6. *Annual Report 2023–24*, Procter & Gamble Hygiene and Health Care Limited, https://assets.ctfassets.net/oe48y40ukei6/7aXOHTgxcGULOBM2hYlblW/6ef76eff5f3da3ecad126944fbaf3391/PGHH_ANNUAL_REPORT_2024.pdf, accessed on 2 April 2025.

4

FROOTI: A DRINK YOU CAN CARRY ANYWHERE

Technology played a role in the case of Whisper but, as we saw, the team built the brand with deep consumer research and insights, and creative communication. Bharat Dabholkar, who worked with Frooti, agrees. The ad guru has been part of much brand research and several launches. We are talking to a multi-faceted personality, one who dons many hats, like that of an actor and playwright, amongst others. But today, we are discussing brands.

'There are times when technology can help to not only differentiate but create a product category,' says Bharat. 'And if there is a first-mover advantage, as in the case of Frooti, it becomes a reason to succeed.'

When Parle decided to launch a fruit drink, it had to contend with many issues. There were soft drinks available in bottles, and fruit juices were already in the market. To make a mark, it needed not just a deep understanding of the gaps in the market and the consumer's mind but also come out with something revolutionary which would immediately attract the attention of the consumer. This is where technology came in.

A fruit drink in a Tetra Pak—combined with great understanding of the consumer need—has seen Frooti remain at the top since its launch more than thirty-five years ago.

It was in 1985 that Parle Agro decided to enter the fruit beverage market. The market then consisted of aerated drinks and some fruit juices, but all of them were available in glass bottles. This meant the customer had to either consume the drink at the shop or come back to return the bottle later. Research showed that the customer was looking for a pack which she didn't have to return. Something she could carry around and dispose later when the drink was finished.

This is where the choice of Tetra Pak packaging came in. The solution was technological but it was the result of research which showed the pain point of a consumer and the convenience offered.

Mango was the natural choice for flavour as Indians love the fruit, and in Mumbai and Gujarat, mango juice and aam ras were popular.

'The nation's love for the fruit is well-known, and when we decided to get into the fruit-juice business, we were sure it would be with a mango drink,' says Prakash Chauhan, chairman, Parle Agro.[1]

The company's research department came up with a product which satiated the consumer's craving for mangoes in seasons when it was not easily available.

Says Bharat Dabholkar, who was with daCunha Communications then:

> The tag line—'Mango Frooti, Fresh and Juicy'—resonated with the customer as it was clear what the drink was about. But the hero was the packaging. No one had had a drink in a Tetra Pak before. The only Tetra Pak [in the market] then was

---

1. Preethi Chamikutty, 'Frooti—A product that has satiated Indian consumer's craving for mango', *The Economic Times*, last updated 25 June 2011, https://economictimes.indiatimes.com/frooti-a-product-that-has-satiated-indian-consumers-craving-for-mango/articleshow/8941829.cms?from=mdr, accessed on 2 April 2025.

> Amul's ultra-high treated milk [UHT] which came in a conical pack and could stay without refrigeration for ninety days. At daCunha, we were working with Amul and were familiar with the packaging.
>
> There were mango drinks like Mangola and Maaza. In fact, Maaza came from the Parle stable, run by Prakash Chauhan's cousin. [Prakash Chauhan is the founder of Parle Agro while his cousin Ramesh Chauhan is the chairman of Bisleri International, which had earlier launched Maaza and Thums Up, a story we shall explore later in chapter 25 of the book.] The drinks came in glass bottles, just like other aerated drinks. The idea was thus to differentiate Frooti by offering it in a different pack. The early ads of Frooti were all about informing the customer.

Parle did customer surveys to find what could be the potential resistance to such a pack. Bharat Dabholkar continues:

> Nobody had seen anything like that before, where you could punch a straw into the pack and walk away with it. With a botted drink, one had to leave a deposit and then return the bottle. Our research showed the customer felt that the packet looked deceptively small. The bottle looked bigger, despite being similar in volume. Our campaign had to be entirely different: [We had to show] that it was mango, it was fresh, the pack could be thrown away and that it had enough volume, it could be chilled.

A good communication model is one which answers all the doubts the consumer may have. But just communication was not enough. There was a need to create a buzz around the launch. Bharat reminisces:

> Parle launched Frooti with a lot of local gimmicks; there were packs of Frooti hanging from trees which people could pluck.

> In stores, standees and promotions were very eye-catching and the curiosity that the pack generated was overwhelming. People who travelled to Mumbai were seen carrying four or five cartons of Frooti with them back home. The point of purchase was the single-most important thing for Frooti, and the drama we generated got us all the attention. The company also did school launches for the brand and every major school in Mumbai stocked Frooti in its canteens. The name suggested was Frooti, because the company had considered extending the name to other fruit drinks as well, not just mango.

The Frooti ad made sure to clarify the customer's doubts about the volume of liquid the Tetra Pak could hold. The agency created an ad in which the customer pours a Tetra Pak of Frooti into a bottle and throws the pack into a dustbin. This solved two perceptions. It clarified the volume contained in the Tetra Pak and also the fact that the pack could be thrown away. The advertisement also showed a customer shivering after drinking Frooti—thus showing the pack could retain a cold temperature!

'Product advertising played a huge role in building the brand; there was a lot of education involved. When Frooti first came out, people mistook it for a soap; we had to tell them to take a straw, pierce it and sip it,' says Nadia Chauhan,[2] the joint managing director and chief marketing officer of Parle Agro.

Frooti was a runaway success, and many other companies launched similar products, but none succeeded. Says a fan, 'Frooti became synonymous with mango drinks. People said, "Godrej ka Frooti dena." But they all failed.'

---

2. Preethi Chamikutty, 'Frooti', accessed on 2 April 2025.

Further research showed that while Frooti was doing exceedingly well, it had started becoming associated with young children. Bharat says:

> We wanted to target the youth and make it a fun drink. We had an ad which used phrases like 'freak out' as it was a common phrase with teenagers then. Sipping the drink through a straw was seen as childish and children too wanted to imitate grown-ups. A thirteen-year-old wants to behave like a sixteen-year-old.

Elaborates an ad agency executive who had studied the Frooti campaign on how the company tackled this perception:

> Variants like Yo Frooti, designed with a pull-back strip exposing the mouth of the Tetra Pak, instead of the plastic straw, struck a chord with the youth. It was no more a children's drink alone. The campaign had lines like 'sip it or swig it', thus appealing to both youngsters as well as the youth.

In 2009, the brand was revamped. Explains Nadia Chauhan:

> When Frooti came into existence, it came in as a really contemporary and youthful drink. It was cool to have a Frooti. Even the imagery in Frooti communication was way ahead of anything else Indian society was exposed to. Frooti commercials in [the] early 1980s with pretty girls in miniskirts and hula hoops, the use of computer graphics, people diving into a pool of Frooti, etc., [were things] India hadn't seen before. We realized being cool wasn't alien to Frooti, it was just about reinstating the cool factor.[3]

Market research showed that there was a need to continue with the cool factor, while still engaging with the youth. The campaign 'Why grow up?' was thus created. In the ads, the customer is shown sipping

---

3. Preethi Chamikutty, 'Frooti', accessed on 2 April 2025.

Frooti, sucking it from the pack noisily, without a care in the world. 'We had to find a voice for Frooti that fit its values, and yet was so cool and contemporary that people in their heads said, "Wow! I didn't look at Frooti like that"', says Sajan Raj Kurup, founder and creative chairman, Creativeland Asia.[4] The brand didn't want to give up its association with children—yet, it wanted to involve adults.

'It sounded [like] the most promising bet for the brand because it embodies the spirit of mango. It turns the associations of Frooti with children and childhood on its head, and to its advantage,' says Kurup. In order to maintain brand salience, it was necessary to create a surprise element.

A 'Mango Surprise' campaign was launched in 2010. Parle conducted surprise pranks on people across major metros. Giant mangoes were dropped from trees and 8-foot mangoes (all harmless and made of light material) were rolled down sloping roads on unsuspecting pedestrians. These moments were captured on hidden cameras and later edited to create the brand's television advertisements. It went viral as branded entertainment content. Over 600 mango pranks were played across thirty centres.

Many drinks were now available in PET plastic bottles, which could be thrown away, and Frooti too launched versions in PET bottles.

Frooti's reach in rural areas was still low and it needed a price point which was affordable. Company research showed that people were interested but were not making the buy as the price point was too high. 'Parle copied the shampoo style and created triangle-shaped small packs of Frooti priced at ₹2.50. Called "Magic Frooti", the stock keeping unit [SKU] helped the brand gain entry into a large number of markets in interior India, doing wonders for the brand,' says Bharat Dabholkar.

We have heard that this helped the brand penetrate markets in rural India, though we don't have insights into the actual numbers.

Frooti didn't just have first-mover advantage but it continued to ride on its success by constantly innovating, and keeping its ear to

4. Preethi Chamikutty, 'Frooti', accessed on 2 April 2025.

the ground and listening to the voice of the customer. This is where most competitors have failed and Frooti continues to be a sought-after drink even today, after nearly four decades.

There are great lessons to learn from Frooti. The brand took the first-mover advantage as it was a pioneer in the segment as the first packaged mango drink in India. This creates a market rather than having to compete for market share. This allowed the brand to establish itself as synonymous with mango beverages, gaining an edge over future competitors. Entering a market early and creating a new category can ensure strong brand recall and customer loyalty. Its innovative packaging in Tetra Paks was revolutionary in the 1980s in India. It was perceived as more hygienic and convenient compared to loose or bottled drinks. It thus enhanced convenience and safety, and created a powerful differentiator.

Frooti worked on creating a strong brand identity, with iconic taglines and ads. Campaigns like 'Mango Frooti, Fresh and Juicy' created an emotional and nostalgic connection with consumers. Over time, these ads maintained their relevance with evolving customer preference. It is clear that consistent and relatable branding builds long-term consumer trust and recognition.

Frooti rode on the enormous distribution network of Parle and ensured availability across urban and rural areas. It was present in retail shops, schools and even small kiosks. Clearly, a robust and widespread distribution strategy ensures product availability and drives volume sales.

Frooti's marketing campaigns consistently targeted the younger demographic through vibrant and playful advertising. More recently, it has adopted digital marketing to connect with millennials and Gen Z. Focusing on specific audience segments and evolving marketing strategies with time maintains brand relevance.

All the above elements of marketing, used well, show Frooti in its leadership position even today, decades after its launch.

5

GOODKNIGHT: TACKLING A PERSISTENT PROBLEM

At times, the entrepreneur has to really 'create a market' when the customer is not actively demanding it, or is not aware of a solution that could solve her problems. Vispy and I are camping in his farmhouse in Alibaug. Mosquitoes are everywhere, and each room has a Goodknight machine to keep the critters away.

When it comes to mosquitoes, the market is unlimited. For India, the problem is not going away soon. Mosquitoes continue to be a menace, as in many tropical countries. The brand Goodknight has become generic to the extent that customers may point to a competitor's product while mentioning that they want Goodknight! It is a remarkable story of how an entire market was created by one focused entrepreneur. We decide to meet the man who thought of the problem and then pursued relentlessly to find a solution!

Goodknight, in some sense, is similar to Frooti, where a technological solution and a product completely new for the country was launched. The promoter was taking a risk as the solution was far more expensive compared to burning neem leaves or using a mosquito net, but he was sure that the customer needed something simple and effective. The challenge for Goodknight was to create a category which didn't exist. It meant not only offering a better solution—a better mouse trap, so to say—but also educating the customer about its usage, coupled with an understanding of the gaps which the new product could fulfil.

Let us look at the Goodknight story.

~

R. Mohan, known popularly as 'Goodknight Mohan', is a man of few words. He trashes market research the way it was done in the 1980s, when he launched Goodknight. 'It makes no sense to go to customers or prospective customers with a sheet of paper and ask questions. That is what market research agencies were doing back then. I had to think like a businessman and believe in what I felt was right. And it worked!'

It was his intuitive sense of a consumer's needs versus his wants that made Mohan launch the mosquito repellent in a chip which was inserted in a machine.

'I saw it in Japan and then I wrote to Sumitomo, the company making allethrin,' he says nonchalantly, as if the Japanese chemical giant was waiting for an electronics engineer from Mumbai to ask its permission to import allethrin and then make it in India! To cut a long story short, it surprised Mohan himself when the giant agreed—after a lot of persistence on his part. And Mohan began making his Goodknight mosquito repellent.

'My wife worked in Air India, and I got a free ticket to Japan! The fact that I met the Sumitomo executives in Japan convinced the guys that I was not only keen but I also had the resources—and they agreed! They didn't know I came using a free ticket.' He laughs out loud.

'The market was dominated by mosquito coils then,' explains Mohan. 'There was Tortoise and Rooster, which held half the market share, and then there were the other products like Odomos, and sprays like Baygon and Finit. There were electronic mosquito repellent [EMR] mats like Vape, which we started distributing but found to be ineffective. This is when we decided to start our own brand once we got the chemical from Sumitomo.'

As is the case when one is creating a market, there is limited value for market research. People, when asked, gave opinions to the contrary, and most didn't believe that there was either a need or a market for the product Mohan was talking of.

This was a consistent theme as we researched the book. Many brands are created with the sheer belief the promoter has in them. If the promoter were to ask potential customers, he or she may be led to believe there was no need for their product.

The famous line, possibly apocryphal, about 'everything that can be invented has been invented' is often attributed to Charles H. Duell, the commissioner of the US Patent Office in 1899. But it shows the importance of the promoter's belief in the product without getting swayed by what the market, or anyone else, is saying. And R. Mohan was one such promoter.

'I could see the value in my product and was tremendously excited, but no one else was. Nevertheless, I pursued my dream,' he says. He goes on to quote a bank manager whom he had approached for a loan as he wanted to set up a factory making the machine: 'Who in India would spend a hundred rupees for a mosquito repellent? If you are aiming for the rich, do you think that their air-conditioned rooms are infested with mosquitos? I don't think they will need this product. Then which demographic would opt for this? Look, gentleman, this is not going to work in our country. Hence, I don't think that any bank will provide a loan for this product. Our banking laws are very complicated.'

Mohan persisted, managing to get a loan from a moneylender, and Transelektra Domestic Products Limited was born, entering the market with the brand 'Goodknight'. 'Initially, we had thought of the name Good Night but we added a K to it,' says Mohan. 'It represents the Knight, the warrior who fought mosquitoes.' The pack showed a mother and child in peaceful slumber, and the name drove home the message the brand wished to convey. The first film had the line 'Meethey sapnon ka Goodknight dost.'

Bharat Dabholkar says that Mohan was convinced the future lay in mats and new technology, and not coils, which had many problems. Their study showed that the customer was not at all satisfied with the coils as smoke was a major concern. The other thing was about the coil falling off, not staying stable in the stand and, at times, not burning through the night. It was also dangerous and could lead to fires. All these problems were eliminated with the mats. Mohan designed the product with a chip and an electrical plug-in.

He continues:

> Mohan's genius was that he identified a gap and found a product filling the same. It was an intuitive, simple and direct solution. Even today, the line about no smoke works. It creates an instant appeal in the minds of the customers, as many still burn neem leaves and dhoop sticks to tackle mosquitoes. The smoke factor has been a consistent line which Goodknight has used well.

Explains Bharat Dabholkar: 'We launched the brand with the line, "Na dhuaan na raakh, sapnon ka Goodknight dost." We launched this in multiple languages. Even the brand name Goodknight was clear and direct, that the product helped provide a good night's sleep.'

We see this trend with most intuitive marketers where the brand name is direct and tells the customer what it does.

Mohan explains the logic of the simple branding, 'Generally, design artists try to bring some mystery and creativity into their design. My interest was to make it as simple and understandable to anyone who saw it. The words should be legible for anyone to read.'

The line 'Millions of Indians go to sleep with the two tender words "good night"' was used in multiple languages, creating an instant connect with the customer.

When competition and 'me-too' products began flooding the market, it was important for Goodknight as a leader to not allow the trust to diminish. It came out with a full-page ad in the newspapers with a guarantee which shocked customers. The ad said, 'If you are using any mosquito repellent mats, and if you are not happy with that, just write a letter to us. We will send you six Goodknight mats free. Use that and let us know the result.'

Says Mohan, 'Thousands of letters were received. We sent a thank-you letter to all of them, along with the promised six mats. It helped us regain trust, and the consumers never left us, despite many other brands making tall claims and selling at a lower price.'

He gives another example of building trust:

> This was before customer satisfaction and such buzz words became popular. I got calls from dealers who said that the customer was not sure if the machine was working as the red light was off. We knew that this could be a minor fault but I gave instructions to our marketing team to replace any such machines—no questions asked. My marketing team was shocked as they expected thousands of such customers to return their machines. But I was confident. As I expected, the total number was in a few hundreds and probably less than 0.5 per cent of our sales! But it created a huge confidence in the minds of our customers, that is, the dealers. Keeping your ear to the ground means listening to what the customer means to say and not what he is literally saying.

By the late 1980s, coil sales had fallen and smoke-free mats made up almost 50 per cent of the repellent market. Goodknight sold well across all urban areas or electrified areas that had high mosquito density, aided by a population earning well enough to experiment on innovative products.

This is where Mohan saw another opportunity. He wanted to get into the spray market as there were still many households which didn't want an electric mat and were not happy with the burning coil. Bharat Dabholkar talks of how he launched the campaign in one evening, all while chatting with Mohan.[1]

At times, competition makes a promoter act fast and create a communication line that not only resonates with the customer but also becomes a bestseller as it addresses a real need. In this case, it was about addressing two different pests—mosquitoes and cockroaches—both of which the customer wanted to get rid of.

Says Bharat:

> We were launching our first cockroach repellent, HIT. One day, we were sitting in the Taj Hotel at Colaba for dinner, when we heard that Bayer was launching Baygon in a single spray for both cockroaches and mosquitoes.
>
> We had to act fast. We had created two different products for mosquitoes and cockroaches, as technically, they needed different treatment. In the case of mosquitoes, the aerosol should stay in the air, while in the case of cockroaches, the liquid had to stick to the floor. We thus had two products.

Bharat explains what they did about the question of killing competition with a smart campaign:

> That evening, while having dinner, I wrote the lines on a napkin. The jingle was based on Ashok Kumar's famous song 'Rail Gaadi'. It went something like this: 'Goodnight cockroach, udta cockroach, chalta cockroach, HIT cockroach.' HIT for mosquitoes was black in colour, while for cockroaches it was red. Baygon had launched a two-in-one. Our line

---

1. Mohan entered the coils category as well, upsetting the then market leader, Tortoise, within a short span. Its ten-hour red Jumbo coils and twelve-hour Jumbo coils (the world's longest-lasting coil), introduced later, were primarily aimed at the rural market.

> 'Kitanuo mein hai farak zameen aasmaan ka' resonated well with the customer and clarified that she needed two different products for cockroach and mosquitoes, and that one didn't work for the other.

The campaign was a hit—as were the sales, which rocketed.

It takes an astute promoter, with a clear understanding of what resonates with a customer, to come up with unique and appealing—sometimes shocking but effective—communication. Mohan talks of an innovative ad which was part of a print campaign. He explains:

> The simplicity in it was about showing a newspaper full of cockroach images almost in 3D. It felt like cockroaches were falling on the paper alongside the line 'cockroach cockroach', while on another white page of the newspaper there was a huge image of a red HIT can with the words 'kills cockroach.' The reader instantly knew that HIT got rid of cockroaches. We also used the words 'Cockroach-free' in some ads as we found that many Jains and others didn't like the word 'kill'.

Continuing on the campaign in the newspaper, the company went for a similar one using buses. 'The bus, on one side, had images of cockroaches and the other side showed "HIT Cockroach" with a white background,' explains Mohan.

By then, the company had been doing exceedingly well in the mats category, but Mohan realized that the client was often confused as to when the mat had finished overnight. It would have turned white from blue and the smell would have disappeared, but that was not enough to tell the customer about its effectiveness.

The role of a promoter is also to remain vigilant about the changes he sees worldwide and introduce the same in his market. Mohan did so by introducing the liquid repellent, which has worked wonders. It also helped solve the customers' problem with the mat repellent. Today, all mosquito repellents come in the liquid-container form.

Mohan's understanding of the market is what got him the leadership position and, soon, other companies were vying to buy him out. He, too, was ready to sell as he had other plans for his life.

In 1994, when a deal with Hindustan Lever did not go through, the Mumbai-based Godrej Group stepped in and acquired Mohan's company. This also marked Godrej's first acquisition. It was reportedly the first time an Indian FMCG company had engaged in a buyout. 'I think our sales was nearly ₹100 crore then,' recalls Mohan.

Today, thirty years later, Godrej continues to innovate to keep the brand relevant and retain its top position.

The Goodknight product range today comprises its latest product, the neem agarbatti, along with the Power Chip System, the Power Active+ System, patches, fabric roll-on, the Xpress System (a liquid vaporizer and diffusing machine), Cool Gel, Power Shots, Activ+, Low-Smoke Coil, the Mini Jumbo Coil and the Fast Card. Goodknight's R&D department is responsible for several breakthrough innovations like the Fast Card—a small piece of paper that is burnt to instantly get rid of mosquitoes and keep them away for about four hours, priced at just ₹1; the Activ+ System that delivers double the power and effectiveness; the Xpress System that works three times faster; the Low-Smoke Coil that reduces smoke; and the neem agarbatti, with neem and turmeric, both natural mosquito repellents.

On Mothers' Day, Goodknight started a campaign with a video showing how a mother knows everything before her family calls out to her for help and how they are always in 'Active Mode'. With the tagline #MomsOnActivMode, the video features two kids talking about how their mom is ever so active while the voiceover of their father jovially asks them how they felt about their mom. While launching Fast Card, Goodknight created a campaign to show consumers that these cards ward off mosquitoes within moments and kids can study without the worry of being bitten. The video features two kids studying in front of their tutor and, as one boy gets distracted again and again by the mosquitoes and gets chided by the tutor, the mother burns the Fast Card and restores his concentration.

A Nielsen survey across sixteen Indian cities in 2015 showed that as many as 77 per cent of the respondents believed that 'dengue' mosquito bites occurred in the night. Godrej started a campaign in schools to increase children's awareness. 'Children are the biggest influencers in the family. Considering there is ignorance about the dengue mosquito—consumers presume that just like the malaria mosquito, it comes in the evenings—it is important that the myths are addressed,' says Sunil Kataria, the business head of the brand back in 2015.[2]

The 'Subah Bolo Goodknight' campaign was a significant advertisement to spread awareness about dengue, which is caused from mosquito bites during the daytime. The advertisement shows a little kid instructing his elder sister to keep the windows closed and take precautions with Goodknight refill machines.

In a campaign related to Goodknight Advanced Xpress System, a mother is seen juggling between adjusting her son's Ravana fancy-dress costume and fumbling with ineffective measures to eradicate mosquitoes. The message here was that instead of installing repellents in instalments, it would be better to get the Advanced Xpress once and for all.

What was established by R. Mohan remains a big hit in the Godrej stable. It continues to innovate, and its R&D centre is a hub of

---

2. 'Mosquito repellent makers Like Godrej Consumer Products, Piramal Enterprise take dengue campaigns to school', *The Economic Times*, 28 October 2015, https://economictimes.indiatimes.com/industry/services/advertising/mosquito-repellent-makers-like-godrej-consumer-products-piramal-enterprise-take-dengue-campaigns-to-schools/articleshow/49560820.cms, accessed on 4 April 2025.

activity, with mosquitoes and other insects buzzing around, testing for the effectiveness of the chemicals used.[3]

Says a senior executive from an ad agency, 'Research showed that consumers buy the refill the most. Godrej faced a problem when Jyothy Laboratories launched a refill cartridge with the promise that it could fit into any machine. Godrej was quick to change its machine to ensure that only its own cartridge fitted into the system. That way the company continued to maintain its leadership position.'[4]

The introduction of Goodknight mosquito repellents, especially its pioneering product lines, offers valuable lessons in product innovation, marketing strategy and consumer-centric branding. Mohan identified consumer pain points, recognizing the widespread annoyance and health risks posed by mosquitoes in India, and developed solutions tailored to different consumer needs (e.g., coils, mats, liquids and later advanced products like natural oils and wearable repellents). He continuously focused on innovation to stay ahead of competitors. For example, Goodknight transitioned to liquid vaporizers, making the product safer, more effective and convenient for indoor use. More recently, Godrej, continuing the same trend, has introduced products like fabric roll-ons and patches, catering to outdoor needs.

---

3. Goodknight is a ₹1000-crore-plus brand, while HIT brings in between ₹500 and ₹1000 crore, as per Godrej's *2024 Annual Report*, https://godrejcp.com/annual-report/2023-24, accessed on 2 April 2025. Man's battle against the mosquito and the beginnings of the Godrej empire coincided. The same year that Godrej & Boyce was incorporated, 1897, Ronald Ross, an India-born British officer serving in the Indian Medical Service proved that *Anopheles* mosquitoes were responsible for the spread of malaria. Ross was awarded the Nobel Prize for physiology in 1902. The battle against malaria (and mosquitoes) had begun.

4 It was the brand All Out, launched by the Arya brothers (through their company Karamchand Appliances Private Limited, or KAPL), which was the first to introduce liquid vaporizers to the market. KAPL was acquired by SC Johnson and then subsequently sold to Bansk, a private equity firm.

Mohan understood the value of effective branding, building trust and recognition through consistent branding. Goodknight positioned itself as a reliable and safe brand, emphasizing family health and well-being. The name 'Goodknight' evokes safety and a peaceful night's sleep, resonating emotionally with consumers. The advertisements too reiterated the same, tailoring the lines to local languages. Like we see in the case of Whisper, Goodknight, too, reached out to consumers to educate them, and often tied its marketing campaigns to awareness of mosquito-borne diseases, like malaria and dengue, positioning the brand as part of the solution to these health issues. Goodknight's ads often focused on family safety, depicting parents protecting their children from mosquitoes, which reinforced the brand's association with care and responsibility.

Mohan was aware of how technology could play a role in buyer behaviour. The small red lamp signifying that the machine is working is a simple yet effective example of understanding the consumer's mind. Goodknight introduced smart plug-in devices with adjustable modes to optimize mosquito protection based on room size and mosquito density. The brand didn't forget adapting to changing preferences, evolving consumer trends and environmental concerns. One example is how the brand is now offering natural and plant-based repellents, thus tapping into the growing demand for sustainable and chemical-free solutions.

Goodknight's success is a result of its customer-focused innovation, effective branding and market adaptability. Companies can learn to prioritize consumer needs, invest in research and development and build a brand narrative that resonates with trust, safety and convenience.

Mohan sums up the journey of Goodknight well. It is a clear reflection of what an entrepreneur can do when it comes to creating a market. He says, 'It started with just a mosquito bite! A simple search of a father to save his daughter from mosquito bites created this leading brand with lasting impact, leading to a new, innovative category in Indian consumer product history.'

6

GLUCON-D: RE-ENERGIZING A BRAND, AND A MARKET

Unlike the story of Goodknight—which built a completely new market—there can be instances where a brand leader needs to go back to the market to understand the gaps and come back with those insights to create a much larger market than ever before.

'I stumbled upon the story when I was conducting research for a talcum-powder brand in Kolkata in the summer. It was extremely hot and we were sweating after just five minutes of walking in the sultry weather. Our hostess, one kind lady named Mrs Ray, gave us a glass of water with Glucon-D mixed in it. It provided instant relief!' Vispy chuckles as he recalls the day. This is when we contacted the ad guru, and a friend, Arvind Sharma, who has more than four decades of experience under his belt, to tell us the story of Glucon-D

Says Arvind, 'At times, a flagging market needs not only the repositioning of a brand but also the activation of dormant needs to expand the market. The case of Glucon-D is striking in the way it not only revamped the market but continued to dominate the same for past three decades.'

It was a problem the company was facing—a brand which had been a cash cow was no longer growing. What could the company do to revive the brand? It needed an examination of the market once more and the studying of consumer behaviour.

This is what Glaxo did. Let us look at the story of Glucon-D.

'The entire category of glucose powder was stagnant, rather, degrowing,' begins Rajiv Sharma, who, like Arvind, was with Leo Burnett when Glaxo approached them for a strategy to relaunch the brand. This was in the mid-1990s.

'Glucon-D as a product was fantastic. It provided instant energy, but no one bought it on a daily basis. It was associated with illnesses or with sportspersons,' adds Arvind Sharma, who headed Leo Burnett then. 'Heinz had bought Glaxo's consumer brands, of which Glucon-D was one. The product had been around for decades and, now, as the brand was degrowing, Heinz wanted to actually withdraw the brand. I asked for time to do some research and come back to them. Survey after survey had featured Glucon-D at the top or among the top ten trusted brands. That meant there was a lot of consumer conviction. This also meant the brand had tremendous inherent strength. We decided to talk to the heavy users of Glucon-D.'

A simple yet effective way to understand a brand's positioning in the minds of the consumers is to talk to those who are regular users—making repeat purchases and especially those buying in bulk. With time, the position may have changed, and such an exercise is regularly carried out by FMCG companies to understand their brand relevance. It is otherwise very risky if the brand loses its connection. Sales lag behind marketing, and a good marketer is one step ahead of sales.

Arvind went to retail shops and found users who bought Glucon-D in large quantities. The areas selected included cities in West Bengal, Odisha and eastern UP, where there was a lot of consumption.

The agency did its research and concluded that there was a need to change the brand perception from Glucon-D being a therapeutic product to being a necessity. 'Glucon-D was a phenomenal product in the 1950s and 1960s. Sugar was not easily available, and Glucon-D filled the gap of providing clean sugar with some vitamin A and vitamin D. Now, all the juices available had the same vitamins. No doctor was recommending Glucon-D any more,' explains Arvind.

'There was a need to "routinize" the consumption; to make it part of a daily use.' Rajiv gives an example of how Cadbury chocolates were turned into a ritual, a dessert, a product of daily use.

Let's take a detour and look at Cadbury chocolates. Campaigns like 'Kuch Meetha Ho Jaaye' associated Cadbury with celebratory rituals, such as festivals, birthdays and even exam results. Cadbury thus expanded its sales with emotional marketing, tying chocolate consumption to significant life moments. It also positioned chocolate as essential—not just for special events but for small, personal victories or to uplift daily life moments. Cadbury capitalized on the cultural practice of gifting, with products like gift boxes, that became integral to rituals of sharing and expressing affection.

Now, coming back to Glucon-D, here was a market leader whose entire category was degrowing. Glucon-D was also seen as a commodity, as glucose powder. The highest sales were in West Bengal, and the agency decided to get consumer feedback to understand buyer behaviour. The agency found that the users were buying the larger 500-gram packs and, at times, even up to 3 kilograms a month. Kolkata is sultry most of the year and people sweat a lot. Children, especially, fall ill when their salt intake reduces. It was found that a glass of Glucon-D was given to the child when she returned from school or play. The housewife would also ask the husband to have a glass of Glucon-D before stepping out of the house in the hot sun. The idea was that Glucon-D would act as a prevention against sun stroke, as dehydration was a key worry.

The agency wondered if there was any medical evidence that Glucon-D worked this way. The agency found what it was looking for in sports medicine, as all sportspersons had electrolytes, heavy on glucose content, after a rigorous workout. That is because one is most susceptible to infections after an intense workout. However, the legal team was not convinced. 'Heinz still had the "medical company" DNA of Glaxo and didn't want to say that Glucon-D prevented sunstroke,' says Arvind.

The agency then came up with an advertisement where an animated sun is shown draining out the energy from a child, and the moment he or she drinks Glucon-D there is a surge of instant energy. While all the other kids, who are playing outdoors, get exhausted by the sun's heat, the one child who drinks Glucon-D remains extremely fresh and energetic. The ad highlighted that the product not only protects from the sun but can also be used every day. Sales naturally picked up. The northern part of India reels under hot winds in the summer, called 'loo', which can cause intense dehydration. And Glucon-D was the answer. 'The campaign led to an increase of sales by 42 per cent when it was launched,' recalls Arvind. A brand which the company wanted to 'kill' as it was 'not growing' had suddenly become a star! And it has continued to remain so.

The Glucon-D example shows that often market research with consumers who are heavy users uncovers brand attributes which the company itself may not be able to articulate.

Keeping sports and children in mind, the agencies, over the years, have created advertisements for the brand which are seasonal, but very relatable and fun to watch.

When research showed that consumers drink plain water to quench thirst, Glucon-D created a campaign in an effort to change habits. Clearly, drinking water doesn't take care of dehydration or the minerals lost. The campaign, with the line 'Sirf Pani Nahi, Glucon-D Wala Pani', was created to encourage the habit of drinking Glucon-D mixed with water after stepping in from the heat outside.

Mohan Kumar, who was the brand manager of Glucon-D in the late 1980s and early 1990s talks of how local players copied the product:

> We were buying from Anil Starch, and many companies did the same by launching similar products. They offered large margins to retailers, while keeping the same price. They were

> taking advantage of the noise made by Glucon-D. We had to be different. We kept the green paper box of Glucon-D, as it was a differentiator, but we wanted to tell the customer that what he or she buys is Glucon-D, while others are copycats. We wanted to associate something with Glucon-D that would make us stand out. This is where the idea of a freebie came up. We had a spoon, a frisbee, a shaker, many such things which were given free with Glucon-D. Soon, the customer would ask for 'Glucon-D with frisbee', thus preventing the retailer from giving another me-too product. We continued with this for a few years and ensured the competition could never make a dent.

Mohan talks of how the green pack was synonymous with Glucon-D. 'When we launched Glucon-C, it had an orange-colour pack but [it was made in such a way that] the customer was reminded of the green pack. We ensured the packaging was such. It was our USP, and we never deviated from it.'

In the same way, readers may recall the blue pack of Vicks, which continues to be synonymous with the brand even today.

'We continued to focus on customer education as we believed that it was a long-term way to establish the brand in the customer's mind,' says Mohan.

Speaking about an ad campaign, Vikramjeet Singh, chief marketing officer, Kraft Heinz India, says, 'In the summers, heat and high humidity lead to exhaustion. Glucon-D aims to educate the consumers about the benefits of adding Glucon-D to water to quickly restore the lost glucose, minerals and vitamin levels in the body after spending long hours in the sun.'[1]

Glucon-D has continued with the same concept of children and sports, keeping in mind the regularity of the consumption behaviour.

---

1. 'Glucon-D Unveils "Sirf Paani Nahi, Glucon-D Wala Paani"', Campaign via McCann, Branding in Asia, 2 May 2017, https://www.brandinginasia.com/mccann-worldgroup-india/, accessed on 2 April 2025.

The idea was to create another behaviour change where the customer was drinking Glucon-D before stepping out as compared to having the drink after a match or returning from the heat. This was another attempt to increase consumption. Research showed that there was a need to protect oneself from the heat even before stepping out. Explains an ad professional:

> Glucon-D has always had loyal customers across India. Through this campaign, the idea was to offer a fresher perspective of the brand narrative from rejuvenation to prevention. The aim was to communicate the importance of being well hydrated with body glucose for lasting energy levels before one ventured out in the sun on a hot day.

In this campaign, a girl, before stepping out of her home, drinks a glass of Glucon-D and goes out to play in the scorching summer heat. While all her other friends are drained out because of the heat, she is still hydrated, pumped up and ready to play even when the sun is shining down brightly! The tagline of this campaign was 'Glucon-D Laga, Energy Chadha.'

The brand changed hands once again, with Zydus Wellness buying it, but the campaign and its focus has remained the same. Tarun Arora, CEO, Zydus Wellness, says that the brand continues to hold 58 per cent market share. 'To unlock the potential, we are focusing on driving daily relevance for the category, so that its usage is not only restricted to the summer or with extreme exhaustion.'[2]

---

2. Rasika Kiran Upasani, 'With 13% penetration, Glucon-D shows huge potential to grow across all markets in India', Exchange4Media, 30 April 2021, https://www.exchange4media.com/advertising-news/with-13-penetration-glucon-d-has-huge-potential-to-grow-across-all-markets-in-india-112664.html, accessed on 2 April 2025.

To continue staying relevant, the company launched a new campaign with the actor Pankaj Tripathi to inject humour into the ads. Explains an ad professional:

> Through the new campaign, with the tagline 'Glucon-D De Energy Satasat, Game Mein Lautaye Fatafat,' the brand wants to highlight how Glucon-D provides energy quicker than any other drink, so that one can bounce back instantly and grab every opportunity through the day. By depicting situations that cause exhaustion, which consumers face on a regular basis, the brand is also trying to build relevance with daily tiredness to drive greater penetration among consumers.

One of the ads shows wedding preparations mounting where Tripathi and the planner are tired of managing all the work in the middle of a sunny afternoon. Out of exhaustion, while Tripathi prefers to take rest, the planner takes out her Glucon-D drink for an instant boost of energy to get back to work so that she can deliver in the best possible way to get more opportunities. Another ad shows a kid playing cricket, with Tripathi as the coach. When Tripathi asks the kid to rest between sessions, he pulls out his Glucon-D instead, which gives him instant energy and allows him to get back to practice and become an all-rounder. Both ads highlight how Glucon-D brings people back to their instant best so they don't have to lose out on opportunities due to everyday moments of tiredness.

Tarun Arora says, 'Glucon-D has always enjoyed top-of-mind recall and is trusted by millions of Indians to provide the instant energy they need. As we look to grow the brand aggressively, we wanted to offer a refreshed brand narrative so we can be a part of people's energy needs, not just in extreme situations like summertime but through their daily routine as well. We are happy to have Pankaj Tripathi on board and are confident that he will help us reach a wider audience and build a deeper connection with every consumer.'[3]

The brand currently has three popular variants: Tangy Orange, Nimbu Pani and Regular. As a part of the brand's extension plans, and following the increased focus on immunity building driven by the Covid-19 pandemic, the brand also launched Glucon-D ImmunoVolt, tasty energy bites for boosting immunity among kids, in 2022.

It continues to lead the market with a 59.5 per cent market share.[4]

The success of Glucon-D is an important lesson in product positioning and discovering unspoken consumer needs. With research, Glucon-D uncovered a real need—that of an energy boost in hot, humid climate. Glucon-D was then marketed as an instant energy drink to combat heat fatigue and dehydration, making it especially relevant for India's hot and humid climate. The glucose-based formula ensured rapid energy replenishment, appealing to both active individuals and those needing an immediate pick-me-up. Initially targeted at children for post-play recovery, Glucon-D expanded its appeal to families by associating it with overall health and vitality, and, when positioned as a drink that provides stamina, it gained popularity among sports players, manual labourers and farmers who need sustained energy.

---

3. 'Glucon-D emphasises the brand's core purpose of providing "instant energy" in new spot', Best Media Info, 12 April 2021, https://bestmediainfo.com/2021/04/glucon-d-emphasises-the-brand-s-core-purpose-of-providing-instant-energy-in-new-spot, accessed on 2 April 2025.
4. 'Zydus Wellness Ltd Q4 Net Sales up by 9.6% to Rs. 778 crores', Zydus Wellness, 14 May 2024, https://www.zyduslife.com/investor/admin/uploads/21/83/Zydus-Wellness-Ltd-Q4-Net-Sales-up-by-9-6--to-Rs--778-crores.pdf, accessed on 2 April 2025.

Glucon-D, as we saw earlier, had a very strong brand positioning, which was reinforced with taglines such as 'Energy ka instant Dose', reinforcing its primary benefit, and became a memorable branding hook. There had always been ease of use, as Glucon-D easily dissolves in a glass of water, and while the original flavour catered to functional needs, later introductions like orange, lemon and tangy mango made it more appealing to children and young adults. The inclusion of essential vitamins and minerals positioned Glucon-D as not just an energy drink but a health booster.

Family-oriented messaging helped Glucon-D associate itself with showing care for loved ones; how mothers ensure their children stay energetic or how workers stay productive for their families. Glucon-D has travelled a long distance from being a brand and product associated with energy but used only in emergencies to becoming something consumers reach for regularly out of habit. It has been a classic case of understanding a consumer's latent needs and highlighting them to drive and change behaviour.

Glucon-D has constantly used insights to create newer ways to change consumer behaviour. And it has worked! It continues to re-energize the company's bottom line.

7

COLDARIN: KUCH LETE KYUN NAHIN?

Creating an entire category from a brand is, at times, needed to shake the market. This is what Arvind Sharma and his team did when they were presented with Coldarin. While not a leader today, let us understand how research helped consolidate Coldarin's brand positioning and make it a brand leader.

While at lunch in the beautiful Royal Bombay Yacht Club, the ad guru recalls a few examples of how insights have been used effectively by brands. Arvind has been around for decades and has many stories to share. We discuss how Darshan Patel, with whom Vispy and team have conducted extensive studies in consumer insights and behaviour, had launched Stopache, an analgesic. It was all about uncovering the unsaid need. In the focus groups which Vispy and his team gather at Ormax Consultants, one can see that the customer says something but means something else entirely. The astute researcher knows how to read between the lines and uncover these hidden needs.

The challenge the brand manager faced was to understand what exactly the consumer—in this case, one suffering from a cold and cough—was looking for. Arvind says, 'Coldarin is a fascinating story about the difference between research and insight. Those days,

Coldarin was with Boots Pharma, and they had done lot of research to understand what Coldarin users were doing. But there was no conclusion, as all that the research did was throw around a lot of data. One has to typically go beyond data to understand what the customer is saying.' He further explains:

> Some of the statements put forth by the consumers were: *When I have a cold I cannot focus completely. Everybody thinks I'm putting on an act.*
>
> *When I have a cold, I cannot stay at home because it's not serious enough. At the same time, I cannot go to office either because I am unable to work there.*
>
> *When I have a cold, I cannot use balm and go to work.*
>
> *When I have a cold, my capabilities are reduced.*
>
> We tried to figure out what all this added up to in a human sense. By then, it was beginning to emerge in my head that it was mostly about the difficulty of being effective at work while labouring through a cold; nobody really sympathizes because it is such a minor condition.

The creative team then went about using this insight to create a film, which many people remember even today.[1] 'The finding was clear,' says Arvind. 'When you have a cold, nobody empathizes with you because it is not a big problem, but you just cannot focus. And Coldarin gets rid of all the symptoms and helps you focus on work. "Sardi se aaram, chusti se chale kaam" was the slogan.'

The ad shows a person suffering from a miserable cold, when his boss comes in and asks, 'Yeh kya haal bana rakha hai? Kuch lete kyun nahin?' And then he says, 'Coldarin ke vishesh tatvon se, sardi se aaram, chusti se chale kaam.' The ads were a big hit as they resonated with the problems and sufferings of a person suffering from a bad

1. Marketing guru Ambi Parameswaran tells us that the company had engaged psychologists in the research, while the ad film was made by Prahlad Kakkar.

cold. Arvind adds, 'It was clear from the ad that if you had a cold, no one would recommend a tablet for headache, but would instead ask you to take Coldarin. The brand created a category out of a simple product, and it remained a leader for decades.'

As we saw earlier, it was a dominant brand like Vicks, with its Vicks Action 500, which usurped the cold and flu market. But Coldarin remains a hero for how insights can be uncovered from raw data. The brand, while not a leader today, is still a dominant one. It has also changed hands many times.

There are many lessons to learn from the story of Coldarin.

Coldarin was solving a common problem targeting one of the most common ailments—colds and flu. Its positioning as a quick-relief solution resonated with a broad audience. By offering a multi-symptom approach (targeting congestion, headaches, body aches and sneezing), Coldarin provided a one-stop solution, eliminating the need for multiple medications. (It is an effective formulation, for those interested in the technical details—Coldarin combines ingredients like paracetamol [for fever and pain], phenylephrine [decongestant] and chlorpheniramine [antihistamine] for comprehensive relief.) Its promise of quick and sustained symptom relief earned it a loyal consumer base. Initial recommendations from doctors and pharmacists helped establish further credibility.

Coldarin ads often emphasized the importance of staying active and productive despite cold symptoms, resonating with working professionals and homemakers. The campaigns highlighted its ability to relieve cold symptoms quickly, a critical factor for consumers seeking immediate relief.

In conclusion, the Coldarin brand's success lies in its effective product formulation, strategic marketing and consistent focus on consumer needs.

By positioning itself as a reliable, fast-acting solution for cold and flu symptoms, Coldarin cemented its place as a go-to brand in its segment.

8

NYCIL: KARO GHAMORIYON KI CHHUTTI

We were in Kolkata when we stumbled upon the story of Glucon-D. It was here that Vispy and his team had done work for a talcum-powder brand. In the hot climes of Kolkata, Chennai and Mumbai, where the humidity levels are also very high, a simple talc doesn't work, as the consumer is looking for a solution to a far more serious problem—prickly heat!

When Glaxo was studying the market for Nycil, the challenge was to find that sweet spot in the consumer's mind which would resonate with the brand's properties and thus make it the default brand. For a brand to succeed, it needs to thoroughly impress upon consumers that it alone is the solution to their problems and nothing else will do. A leader brand is then established.

To understand the story of Nycil better, we return to Arvind Sharma for the details.

Another brand from the Glaxo stable, which was bought by Heinz, is Nycil, an anti-mycotic powder meant to prevent fungus. It was meant originally for a condition called athlete's foot. Darshan Patel of Paras Pharma later came up with Dermicool. Nycil was sprayed between the toes to prevent fungus. 'The brand got repositioned for prickly heat somewhere in the mid-seventies,' Arvind tells us. Predictably, the brand's advertisement in print said very little. The brand was moving slowly, though they had the correct insight that prickly heat was where most fungal infections occur. Scratching the prickly-heat spots leads to a fungal infection and hence Nycil was the right product. According to Arvind:

> In the late 1970s, Nycil was seen as a promising brand, but it was moving very slowly. Glaxo used to carry out something called a 'Habits and Practices' study every few years, to uncover the surrounding space of any brand. The Nycil study was about talcum powder and other surrounding data. I looked at the data and realized that the consumption of prickly heat powder was 60 per cent amongst women, under 30 per cent for children and a very small percentage for men. The data was part of a large report, a few hundred pages thick, and the marketing manager would rarely use the data to come up with a campaign. In reality, the insights gleaned from the report were not used. I asked why women are such a large customer segment and the response was that women work in kitchens where the heat is intense. I probed further to understand the exact usage. The ad agency was clear that they wanted to shoot a woman's back in the television commercial or print ad, as no one wanted to see a man's back. My pushback was that children play in the heat outside and that they can suffer from prickly heat as much as women, or possibly more.

He further explains, 'The insight was simple—all of us are more bothered about the pain and discomfort of children … Much more than anything else. Who can neglect a child who is suffering?'

We have seen used in the Vicks ad the concept of mother's love, and it continues to work for the brand, as it has for Maggi noodles. The Nycil data suggested otherwise—the users were largely women.

'And this is where the insights differ from what the data shows,' says Arvind. While a marketer would have continued to focus on women, the intuitive researcher realized that children's problems were larger but were not being seen.

Luckily, the Nycil management understood this and greenlit an advertisement that became an instant hit.

The Nycil advertisement showed a young boy with a thorn bush growing out of his back, symbolizing the itchiness, irritation and discomfort of prickly heat. The visual emphasized on how prickly heat feels unbearable. The ad then shows Nycil being applied, with the soothing action of the product metaphorically removing the 'thorns' and bringing instant relief to the boy.

To highlight the cooling effect brought about by Nycil, the brand tried some interesting experiments. The Nycil 'Cooling Bus Stop' ad campaign was a health-related ambient-medium campaign that took place in July 2009 in Kolkata. An air cooler was placed at a city bus stop to demonstrate the cooling effect of Nycil Prickly Heat Powder. Bus-stop advertising can be an effective way to reach a large number of people in a specific geographical area. Bus-shelter posters are also a good local campaigning tool because they are affordable and can be tailored to be more relevant in different locations.

In another ad, a young girl is urging a boy to play outdoors while he suggests indoor games and continues to scratch his back uncomfortably. The respective mothers look concerned when one of them suggests Nycil. She dismisses 'ordinary powders', saying only Nycil will work. And then the mother talks of the 'clinically proven formula' with the power of neem, which is effective in providing relief to 'ghamoriyan', or prickly heat. In another ad, a wife returns from a work trip to find her husband and children playing indoors. When asked why, the son says it is because of prickly heat. The husband says he tried talcum powder, but it didn't work. This time, the wife talks about how only Nycil will work and the pack she displays has the words 'Germ Expert' prominently displayed—giving an assurance of a relief.

A mother couldn't see her child suffering. 'A child's discomfort is a far bigger pain than your own,' says Arvind. 'Nycil dramatically improved in sales and the brand grew. The entire category grew. Today, in the period between March and October, between summers and the monsoon, most households stock up on prickly heat powder. The brand grew by nearly 15–20 per cent. Her silhouette vanished from the ads after that. And the visual of the child's back afflicted with prickly heat has been a constant for Nycil.'

Today, the brand is owned by Zydus Wellness.[1] Both Glucon-D and Nycil, part of Zydus's stable, are leaders. Glucon-D has a market share of 59.5 per cent and has maintained its number-one position. Nycil has maintained its dominant position and now stands at 35 per cent in the prickly-heat-powder category.[2]

The success of Nycil Prickly Heat Powder lies in its ability to address a specific and common problem—prickly heat and sweat-related skin irritation—especially in tropical climates like India. Nycil provided an effective solution for a specific problem, thus avoiding competition with ordinary talc. Its anti-bacterial properties, with its active ingredient, chlorphenesin, offered relief from itchiness and prevented bacterial infections caused by excessive sweating. The talc-based formula delivered a soothing, cooling effect on the skin, offering immediate comfort in harsh weather. Over time, Nycil introduced variants with added benefits, such as aloe vera for moisturizing and sandalwood for a natural fragrance, catering to different preferences.

---

1. Zydus Wellness did not buy Glaxo brands, but it did acquire the India businesses of Kraft Heinz in 2018, which included brands like Complan, Glucon-D and Nycil.

2 'Zydus Wellness Ltd Q4 Net Sales up by 9.6% to Rs. 778 crores', Zydus Wellness, 14 May 2024, https://zyduslife.com/investor/admin/uploads/21/83/ Zydus-Wellness-Ltd-Q4-Net-Sales-up-by-9-6--to-Rs--778-crores. pdf, accessed on 2 April 2025.

Strong brand positioning has ensured its position as a must-have product during the summer, thus tapping into Indians' seasonal need for skin protection and comfort. Visual storytelling and memorable advertisements (for instance, the bramble on the boy's back) has been another reason for its success. The ads often featured mothers caring for their children, appealing emotionally to protection and care.

In summary, Nycil's success stems from its problem-solving formulation, targeted marketing and consistent focus on providing value to consumers. It has transformed itself into a summer essential, earning trust and loyalty across generations.

The story of Nycil also tells us how data can be easily misread, and how reading it correctly can lead to a successful communication and positioning strategy. Once more, focusing on children and tapping into mothers' concern and love has worked.

'Consumer insight needs to be leveraged—the way Nycil did,' says Arvind, as he dives into anecdotes from the early days of FMCG marketing. When speaking with an ad professional boasting of over four decades of experience, tangential brand stories are inevitable. Here, we explore some compelling nuggets—not full-blown case studies but illuminating examples of how consumer insights have shaped iconic brands.

Arvind recalls Aspi Balsara, of Balsara Hygiene, who was a master at identifying market gaps and positioning products strategically. Aspi began with household staples like Odomos, India's first mosquito repellent, and Odonil, a pioneer in air fresheners. Today, under Dabur's stewardship, Odomos has evolved to include creams, gels, lotions and even wearable patches. Similarly, Odonil, launched in 1972, was repositioned from being a simple washroom freshener to a mood enhancer. With its memorable 'Why Does Our Bathroom Smell Better than Theirs?' campaign, Odonil became a household name, evolving into multiple scented variants. Dabur's marketing muscle extended its reach, securing its leadership in the air-freshener category.

How Odomos and Odonil became brand leaders is a story we have not covered here. For now, we return to Aspi's relentless passion for innovation.

Arvind highlights Aspi's challenge when launching Promise toothpaste. In a market already dominated by Colgate, positioning was critical. Arvind recounts:

> We needed something unique. Research revealed that clove oil—a trusted remedy for tooth pain—could be our differentiator. Enter Promise: the toothpaste with clove oil. Its advertising cleverly tapped into nostalgia—a grandmother applying clove oil for toothache—and positioned Promise as a trusted solution. The packaging, with its distinctive green colour and clove imagery, stood out against Colgate's red-and-white branding. Promise soared to a 15 per cent market share, cementing itself as the number-two toothpaste brand, before eventually joining Dabur's portfolio.

As we savour mango desserts, Arvind shifts gears to talk about another success story: Maaza. 'Every Indian loves mangoes,' he says, weaving in the brilliance of Maaza's positioning—authentic mango stories. The ads evoked nostalgia: childhood summers, stolen mangoes and a longing for mangoes which are out of season. Maaza's emotional storytelling built a billion-dollar brand for Coca-Cola. Arvind reveals, 'Do you know one of Coke India's major KPIs [key performance indicators] is to grow mango production in the country? That's the power of Maaza!' Research, he adds, showed that 62 per cent of consumers named Maaza as their most-loved soft drink. 'Imagine if Coke had supported Maaza like Coca-Cola itself—it could have dominated the market.'

Arvind then shares the curious tale of Meswak toothpaste, another of Balsara's innovations. Targeting the Muslim community, Meswak leveraged its mention in the Quran for dental hygiene. However, Arvind reveals, 'Most Muslims didn't know about this reference and Hindus were hesitant to use it.' The initial campaign failed. Market research came to the rescue, uncovering Meswak's Ayurvedic benefits: it was an antiseptic and astringent with healing properties. Instead of emphasizing a single benefit, Meswak was positioned as a versatile herbal solution for everyone. A clever series of commercials—where shoppers proudly extol Meswak's myriad benefits—helped the brand take off, capturing a 5 per cent market share with impressive margins. 'It was a cash cow,' says Arvind with a smile, noting Dabur's decision to support Meswak for its profitability.

'Sometimes,' he concludes, 'counterintuitive logic works. All it needs is sharp insight and unwavering commitment from the brand owner.'

9

JOCKEY: GETTING THE UNDERWEAR OUT OF THE CLOSET

Consumer insight is all about trying to understand what the customer truly needs or aspires for but is not able to—or does not want to—articulate. Many brands or products in India are aspirational, and there is a huge market if the brand is made available at the right price and value for the Indian customer. Innerwear brands were largely ignored in India as they were not considered 'fashion'. It was a category waiting to be exploited. In the early 1990s, with liberalization, Indian customers were getting exposed to foreign brands and aspired to get their hands on some of them. They just needed someone to make it available to them.

The same thought occurred to Sunder Genomal, an entrepreneur from the Philippines, when he studied the innerwear market in India. The fact that, today, Page Industries, the company behind the Jockey brand, is a huge success, might make the story seem simple. But that was not the case when it all began. The key issue facing Jockey was creating a market for high-quality innerwear. It was an opportunity, no doubt, but also quite a challenge as it required a clear study of the market, a proper understanding of the gaps in it, understanding customer aspirations and then creating a communication strategy to address the same. Jockey had a high-quality product, successful internationally—but selling in India and reaching leadership levels seemed to require a different approach than what worked elsewhere.

The innerwear market has been dominated by Indian brands, and as far as television advertising is concerned, almost every top Bollywood star has been seen promoting some brand or the other. And with them being stars, the product advertised is a vest, not underwear, in most cases. The taboo, in some sense, continues.

The Jockey story is about its entry into the Indian market in 1994 and how it changed the rules of the game entirely, with the brand continuing to dominate the scene even thirty years later. Jockey has almost no competition in the premium segment, despite many international brands being available in India now. 'While the underwear and innerwear market is huge, there is no clear syndicated data to verify the numbers,' says Karthik Yathindra, then chief marketing officer of Jockey in India; he was elevated to CEO in 2025. He adds, as an aside, 'The company, Jockey International Inc., had entered India for the first time in 1962. However, at that time, it faced an unexpected exit from India due to regulatory hurdles. Either way, Jockey is not competing with other brands in the market, and has clearly created a market where none existed before. It found a gap and has managed to perch itself at the top there since its launch.'

The Genomals, a Sindhi family originally from Rawalpindi, Pakistan, had migrated to the Philippines and were associated with the Jockey brand for nearly fifty years. When Sunder Genomal, the grandson of the founder, was given a chance by Jockey International to open a manufacturing set-up in India in 1994, he first commissioned a survey to understand the market. Innerwear was sold as a secondary product, never displayed prominently in shops. Most shopkeepers, when asked for underwear, either male or female, would take the products out of a shoe box or a similar kind of carton, often kept below the counter. It was almost an apology of a sale. Never was the product considered interesting enough to be displayed prominently in the storefront.

'For decades,' agrees Sunil Sethi, executive chairman, Modenik, the makers of the Dixcy Scott brand of innerwear, 'very little had changed in the men's mass innerwear market. Men—or more often, their mothers and wives—went into hosiery shops, mentioned the size they needed and then chose from the boxes the shopkeeper placed in front of them. They didn't ask questions beyond enquiring about the quality of the elastic.'[1]

Sunder Genomal realized that there was a need to literally get underwear out of the closet. Also, there was also a clear gap in the quality of the product being sold. Jockey, an international brand, focused on quality, and Page Industries, Sunder's company, which held the franchise for Jockey in India, decided to ensure that the quality of its products was at par with Jockey's international standards.

Market research clearly showed that the customer didn't have too to choose from, and whatever international brands were available in India were more suited to European body types. This was an interesting finding. Page Industries decided to focus on making quality undergarments while keeping in mind the Indian body.

The process of selecting retailers followed the same philosophy of getting the category out of the closet—those retailers who refused to display Jockey products in specified display fixtures were not selected. It was clear that the brand was aspirational, and the company wanted to do everything to ensure the customer desired the product. 'Creating desire was the key to initial success,' a company senior executive says. 'The market was then made of brands like VIP, Tantex, etc., but Jockey didn't consider them as competition as

1. Gowri N. Kishore, 'Dixcy Scott: Addressing the Transitional Indian Man', The Hard Copy, 5 October 2022, https://thehardcopy.co/case-studies-dixcy-scott-addressing-the-indian-transitional-man, accessed on 3 April 2025.

it was priced nearly twice or more than a regular VIP underwear,' explains Karthik. 'We were in the mid-premium segment, outpricing everyone in the market. It was a deliberate strategy in line with our quality offering.' According to him:

> We had a category which was considered 'taboo' to prominently display on store fronts. We wanted to ensure that customers understood that Jockey was a premium international brand with high quality, and we used Caucasian models for our ads. We don't use Bollywood celebrities. Today, most Indian brands like VIP, Lux Cozi, Rupa and Dixcy Scott use Indian film stars. We don't as we feel they don't add value, and it is confusing for the customer. In fact, some stars have changed their brand endorsements over a period of time, leaving the customer confused. I am not sure how it helps the brands. Our products are clearly premium, and we don't see any value in having Bollywood celebs for our promotion.

Jockey's advertisements have always stood out due to their unique approach. Notably, campaigns like 'I'm Feeling Good', 'Jockey or Nothing' and 'Jockey Knows Me' focused on conveying a narrative centred on 'comfort' rather than on traditional themes like 'machoness' or 'seduction'. By strategically aligning Jockey with the shifting societal landscape, Page Industries managed to revolutionize the innerwear market in India, showcasing how even the most concealed and intimate products can acquire aspirational significance.

Today, Jockey is by the far the only player in the mid-premium segment. Karthik tells us:

> Hanes was the only other brand which was focused on innerwear. Other brands like UCLA, US Polo, and many others, are into other garments and have a small segment as innerwear, unlike a focused player like Jockey. Hanes has had

> some business issues in recent years and we don't consider them competition. We have a clear path ahead. We have extended our innerwear line to add comfort wear, which includes loungewear and nightwear. In the women's category, nightwear is clearly differentiated from loungewear, unlike in the men's category. We have also launched products for boys and girls. The women's bra products launched in 2003–04 are also doing extremely well.

Jockey is a classic case of not just succeeding in the marketplace but also becoming a stock market darling. Page Industries, since its debut on the stock market, has given eye-popping returns to shareholders. This is because the investor sees growth potential. According to some estimates, the unorganized market is still more than 70 per cent of the total market. 'But Jockey isn't worried as it does not consider the entire market as the TAM [total addressable market],' explains Karthik. He continues with confidence:

> We have a long way to go. Our total sales are around ₹5000 crore as of March 2023, and we see a huge potential to continue growing further. As we expand to tier 2 and 3 cities, we see a lot of aspirations for customers to not only graduate to this mid-premium segment but the desire to move is also driven by the perception of quality, which is significantly better than Indian innerwear brands.

With the right quality, consistent advertising showcasing its international brand origin and premium but affordable pricing, Jockey has clearly understood the innerwear market. It has not tried to diversify into other areas. A deep understanding of the customer's needs has helped the brand position itself as the go-to product for innerwear.

'Like most entrepreneurs, Sunder Genomal understood intuitively the need to position the product as premium. Many managers would have been tempted to operate in the established market where Indian players were already selling. But Sunderji took the gamble to operate in a blue ocean, and see how it has helped the company,' Karthik says with pride.

There are many lessons to learn from the Jockey success story. Jockey introduced the concept of branded, high-quality innerwear, appealing to aspirational consumers, marketing itself as a premium, international brand, and targeting urban and middle-class consumers who were willing to pay more for quality. Jockey capitalized on the growing disposable income of India's middle class, who sought better quality and branded products. Jockey offered modern designs, superior fits and comfortable fabrics, setting a new benchmark in the Indian market. The brand has continued to innovate regularly, and has introduced new styles and product categories, such as seamless lingerie and athleisure, to keep up with changing trends.

The main theme of Jockey was aspiration, and it positioned itself as youthful, stylish and modern, appealing to India's upwardly mobile population. Ads with taglines like 'Jockey or Nothing' emphasized quality and brand loyalty. By showcasing innerwear as part of a broader lifestyle choice, Jockey moved away from utilitarian perceptions of innerwear. Jockey invested in exclusive brand outlets (EBOs), creating a premium shopping experience for customers. Jockey adapted its product offerings to suit Indian preferences, such as conservative cuts, breathable fabrics for hot climates and affordable price ranges for different income groups. The brand offered a wide range of sizes, ensuring a good fit for diverse body types.

In summary, Jockey's success in India stems from its ability to redefine innerwear as a lifestyle product, backed by quality, strong branding and effective market adaptation. It created a category of aspirational innerwear, transforming consumer perceptions and habits.

Sunder Genomal's story of launching Jockey is similar to that of many Indian entrepreneurs who saw an opportunity not by competing with other brands but by creating an entirely new space, opening new markets and remaining at the top for decades, not only giving spectacular returns to the company but, in the end, providing the right product at the right price at the right quality to the discerning customer. 'The understanding of customer needs and fulfilling the same is after all the true job of a marketer. And we don't rest on our success but carry out research and brand studies every quarter to remain at the top of the game,' concludes Karthik. We couldn't agree more.

While discussing Jockey, it is important to mention another leader brand from the stable of Page Industries.

We are talking about Speedo, which has had literally no competition in the market since Page Industries launched it in India in 2011. It is once again a classic case of 'creating a market'. Explains Karthik:

> Speedo has a mission statement: 'Make India Swim.' We are here to grow the market. India is not a country where millions swim—unlike cricket, which is a very popular sport. But our brand is positioned as a performance brand and not a beachwear or casual-swimwear brand. Like in Jockey's case, Speedo stands for quality at a premium price, and the customer is willing to pay for it.

The brand is being promoted through swim centres and swim clubs. The success of Speedo in India, a global leader in swimwear, can be attributed to its ability to adapt to the unique characteristics of the Indian market while leveraging its strong international reputation. Speedo rode on its international heritage. Its legacy as a trusted swimwear brand, especially for professional swimmers, gave it immediate credibility in India. Despite the country being a small market, Page Industries didn't stop at innovation, and

Speedo introduced advanced swimwear with features like chlorine resistance, quick-drying fabrics and ergonomic designs, catering to both casual swimmers and professionals. Like Jockey, which was meant for Indian body types, Speedo also introduced swimsuits suited to Indian sensibilities, such as full-body swimwear and modest designs, thus appealing to a broader audience. There is a growing swimming culture in India, and Speedo capitalized on this view of swimming as a recreational and fitness activity in urban India, driven by increasing access to swimming pools and awareness of fitness. Quite naturally, Speedo partnered with swimming academies, fitness centres and aquatic-sports-events organizers to solidify its reputation in the niche swimwear segment. Like Jockey, Speedo launched physical stores in key urban markets, offering a premium shopping experience through exclusive brand outlets.

The branding is aspirational, just like Jockey, and Speedo has positioned itself as a high-quality, performance-driven brand, appealing to India's growing middle- and upper-middle-class populations willing to invest in quality products.

While there is still a long way to go, Page Industries' Speedo and Jockey continue to remain leaders with a potential to become much bigger than what they are today. It is an enviable position to be in.

To sum up, Speedo's success in India stems from its premium positioning, product innovation, focus on building a swimming culture and strategic marketing, making it the preferred brand for swimming enthusiasts across the country. Additionally, the brand's alignment with India's growing health and fitness consciousness has driven demand for premium swimwear products.

10

WEIKFIELD: CHANGING TASTES

While, with Jockey, the Genomal family had to literally demand that the product be displayed prominently, in many product categories, the marketer has to carry out live demonstrations to make the customer try and taste the product.

Insights, if rightly used, not only create markets but make brand leaders! We have seen this repeatedly in all the stories we have covered thus far. And we know that changing food habits is one of the most challenging tasks for a marketer. Nestlé brilliantly found a soft spot in mothers and their need to whip up a quick snack for their children returning from school, making Maggi a household name.

Kellogg's suffered for a long time, unable to 'change the breakfast habits of Indians', as they had proclaimed. And when it comes to 'British desserts' like custard, the challenge is even more difficult. However, an astute marketer can make a success of it, with determination, tenacity and 'product sampling' to make people literally try it out.

Food is one of the most challenging spaces for a brand to operate in and succeed. And if the product being launched is one which Indians are not aware of, the challenge is manifold. This was the problem the promoter of a food brand faced when trying to launch his brand in India. It was once more a case of creating a market—from scratch, literally—one customer at a time.

At times, the marketer has to literally demonstrate and handhold, or feed, in this case, for a prospective buyer to create a market. Some products are such that the consumer lacks awareness and a large part of the market segment simply does not know the product. They have never tasted it; hence, they won't buy it even if it is available. Sample testing and tasting has been commonly used for many products, including perfumes. There are many examples from the US. PepsiCo launched a variant of Mountain Dew called Code Red, a cherry-flavoured cola, after sampling and testing different flavours with consumers. The success of the flavour led to its national launch, and it became one of the brand's most popular variants. The ice-cream company Ben & Jerry's is well-known for conducting extensive sampling events, both in-store and at festivals, to introduce new flavours. For example, when launching flavours like 'Cherry Garcia' or 'Half Baked', they first tested them through small sample distributions to gather consumer feedback before going national.

At times, sampling can also lead to negative feedback. We saw earlier how Coke failed when it heard the customer's feedback in blind tests and decided to withdraw its iconic brand.

Nevertheless, sampling allows companies to gather real-time reactions and make necessary improvements to create a product that resonates with a wide audience, ensuring that it will succeed in the competitive marketplace.

In the case of Weikfield, it was all about introducing a product which most customers had possibly heard of but never tasted. This was what Bahri Malhotra was dealing with when he launched Weikfield's custard powder in the mid-1950s. It required sample tasting—and an elaborate one at that!

Coincidentally, like the Genomals, the Malhotras too are a Sindhi family who moved to India from Rawalpindi. They eventually settled down in Pune, showcasing their grit and determination. But that is a story for another day—one captured in the founder's memoirs.

Bahri Malhotra reminisces:

> I travelled continuously—almost 180 to 200 days a year—to introduce the custard to shopkeepers and distributors all over India. Air travel was limited to the wealthy and road travel was not practical back then. So I travelled by the overcrowded second-class train compartments. On reaching my destination, I would book the largest retiring room in the station terminal for my stay. The rooms were well maintained and the cost was low. I would visit the markets, spending the day meeting city traders at their offices and would invite each one to my retiring room for a 'custard cocktail party' in the evening.
>
> I would buy a few cans of mixed fruit—canned cherries, peaches, pineapples or whatever was available. Arriving at the station, I would drop in to the canteen and give the chef there some custard powder, which I always carried in my suitcase for sampling at these parties. For a small fee to cover the cost of milk, sugar, fuel and labour, the canteen would prepare and then serve the custard in my room once the party started. By then, I would be waiting with soft drinks and wafers or chivda for my guests to arrive after they had shut their shops for the day. I would invite them to sample a custard cocktail. This was a delicious concoction of Weikfield vanilla custard poured over chilled canned fruit and a little syrup. Most of the guests had never tasted such a dessert and, being invariably floored by the delicious and creamy taste, would ask for more.

Bahri Malhotra smiles as he adds:

> Some of them waited for real cocktails to arrive, but soon they realized that the pudding was in itself enjoyable, and

the resentment would vanish. I would return a few weeks or months later, and they would turn up again, bringing their friends along, eager for more.

Having tasted the custard cocktail, the traders wanted a continuous supply of it for their own homes. They could definitely see the business potential of our product. The retailers became enthusiastic to stock and sell our custard powder in their shops, and that made it easier to get the wholesale distributors to take interest in stocking our product too.

The lesson we learnt from this was very simple. In the case of food products, fancy words and beautiful images do work, but only up to a point. The real trick lies in trying a few spoonfuls! A taste of our product broke down all resistance, and people knew that they wanted more and had to buy it.

With more than a few hundred custard cocktail parties, I was nicknamed the 'custard cocktail man' by shopkeepers in cities all over India.

Understanding customer need was a crucial aspect of success for Weikfield. Malhotra says, 'When we first began making our custard powder, we had to compete against a well-established multinational company, Brown & Polson. They were importing their custard powder, packing and marketing it in a one-pound tin.'

Malhotra found that the size was not convenient for both a large bakery, which used a lot more custard powder, as well as the domestic user, who needed a much smaller pack which gave them the option of making just the amount required for a family. Weikfield thus created separate packs for institutional as well as retail sales. The new packaging increased the penetration of Weikfield substantially and it has continued to remain a leader in its category.

Understanding the customer segment first, which will be ready to buy the products, is crucial. Says D.S. Sachdeva, aka Dipy, then CEO of Weikfield:

> Custard is a typical British dessert; Indians are not used to it. It was largely popular in the Indian military cantonments and towns which—like the hill stations—were influenced by the British. The army continues to follow many British traditions. Weikfield saw an opportunity to enter the market and beat Polson, which was only available in a large pack and not convenient for a home user. Weikfield was the first to launch custard powder in consumer packs. They added jelly crystals and baking powder, which are all used in custard-based desserts.[1]

Keeping customer preferences in mind, Weikfield launched a vegetarian version of the jelly as many customers didn't want to eat a product which contained gelatine, which is made from animal bones. Explains Malhotra:

> We launched our vegetarian jelly with a hard-hitting campaign occupying prime space in the most widely read magazines of the time [1986]. We had full pages in *Femina* and *Eve's Weekly*, the *Reader's Digest*'s back cover and various other publications whose readers enjoyed Weikfield. We also made it very clear that we were the first and only manufacturer and seller of vegetarian jelly in India. As our campaign continued, confusion in the customers' minds caused the market to initially shrink by about 90 per cent of what it had been. Then our market share began to climb and, soon, about 50 per cent of it was ours. We had quadrupled our sales from a 10 per cent to a 40 per cent market share by introducing our vegetarian jelly!

This helped the company export its products to the Gulf and markets in the Middle East, where the company was unable to source Halal-

1. Sachdeva moved out of Weikfield in June 2024.

certified gelatine. Non-gelatine-based, pure vegetarian jelly crystals solved the problem!

According to Sachdeva:

> The idea of a 'sweet portfolio' was to ensure that we stayed focused in the Western desserts' segment and not get into, say, gulab jamuns and such. We are the number-one player in a not very large market. It is a conscious strategy to operate in niche segments. You must have seen food trucks selling falooda and milkshakes across India? All of them use Weikfield custard powder.

Says Bahri Malhotra, 'Over the years, the Indian army has been a large consumer of our products, through both direct use and sale to officers through the Canteen Stores Department.'

Quite often, the name of the brand plays an important role in its success. In the case of many brands from Paras Pharma, the name is directly linked to the product—for example, Set Wet Gel, Moov or Krack Cream. It directly tells the customer what the product stands for. But in Weikfield's case, it was a different story.

Bahri Malhotra explains why the name 'Weikfield', a foreign-sounding one, was used:

> Weikfield is seen as a trusted and reliable brand, and our products are truly enjoyable. It is assumed that we are a foreign company, perhaps a European one, operating in India. This helped a lot back when we launched the company, as the Indian industry was new and still struggling to achieve quality standards. The really-good-quality products were imported. To be identified so clearly by consumers as a 'foreign' brand was a validation of our quality.
>
> It was clear to the promoters that a name like 'Bharat Custard' or 'Malhotra Custard' would have the discerning buyers of the 1950s turning their noses up at the product, and

the enterprise would have floundered. The name Weikfield, which hinted at European origins, gave the brand an additional touch of authenticity for people with sophisticated palates.

As we have seen with other products, branding, when combined with an understanding of the consumer mindset, is an essential element of success.

Repeatedly, the perceptive marketer understands the gaps in the sector. Market research and the insights derived from them go a long way in establishing the success of a brand, which needs to be nurtured with the right communication, consistent strategy and the right mix of other marketing elements—be it promotion, distribution or sampling.

Weikfield is a classic story of creating a market, one customer at a time, by inducing them to try out the product. We see in the case of Weikfield how an extensive sampling campaign was carried out by the promoter himself, as he was convinced of its eventual popularity. But he didn't stop at that alone and ensured that the product was available too. Bulk sales to government departments like the Canteen Stores Department ensured that it made its way into every military home, and that helped in making the product very popular. Weikfield is available in popular flavours like vanilla, mango and strawberry, thus catering to diverse taste preferences and ensuring wide appeal.

Stories like Weikfield showcase the resilience and conviction of the promoter and his ability to ensure that the product is made widely popular. The fact that it continues to be a leader in its category is no surprise at all.

11

VOLVO BUSES: A TRANSFORMATIVE RIDE

A determined marketer believes in his own insight and conviction, which oftentimes works better than formal market research. This is a recurrent theme in many brand stories. When you believe in a product—which has been successful elsewhere in the world but has no market in India, according to market research—you need to be really convinced and determined to succeed. And go to great lengths to make it happen. In the case of Volvo, there was overwhelming feedback that such a product was not needed in India. This is where the conviction of the marketer is tested—when he goes by what he believes in rather than the feedback received. How does the customer know what he wants unless he has tried out the product? The runaway success of Volvo Buses is the story of a brand asking this very question.

'Let's take a Volvo,' I suggest to Vispy as we make our way to Pune. 'It is better, faster and safer than driving ourselves.'

He agrees and we board the bus at Dadar. Volvo has become synonymous with comfortable travel. Even though, today, there are a few other bus manufacturers who claim to offer similar comfort, Volvo has, by far, been the leader for the past twenty-five years. And to hear the story, we are meeting Akash Passey, who was the first employee of Volvo Buses in India.

In his swanky new office at the German company, ZF Group, we meet Akash, who tells us:

> Volvo came into India with trucks and a big investment of around ₹450 crore to start a factory by mid-1998. There were other divisions, too, like bus, industrial construction and marine. Certain localization was needed for the buses and trucks. Volvo got serious traction in the bus business when the Delhi government announced a tender for 1,500 low-floor buses in 1998. People didn't know what low-floor buses were.

Akash pauses here to tell us an anecdote. 'Many people came to see the Volvo bus at the 1998 Delhi Auto Expo.' He laughs, recalling an animated discussion between two youngsters he overheard. 'The older of the two, in an attempt to explain how the bus loses height, said: "When it halts, the driver jumps out and deflates the tyres."'

Akash came in as employee number one in the Volvo bus division, a young executive in his late twenties. He wondered whether Volvo should work with the government when the Delhi administration floated a tender for buses. Volvo applied for and got a Letter of Intent for 200 buses, but when the government changed, the tender vanished too.

The true grit of a determined marketer is the ability to study the bigger picture and not get enamoured by low-hanging fruit. In the long run, it is the larger market which should serve the brand. And this is what Akash worked towards. He says:

> I studied the long-distance-travel market in India and realized that there were less than fifty air-conditioned buses in operation. Imagine! In the late 1990s, there were just these few air-conditioned buses available for long-distance travel. The maximum horsepower offered by the two existing manufacturers then was 110 HP, which meant an auxiliary unit was needed to provide complete air-conditioning. There was no guarantee of a comfortable ride. Moreover, the bus operator had provided windows similar to that of a non-AC bus. The windows, which were operable like any other bus, made the whole travel experience very unreliable. The comfort promised was missing. With an engine in the front, a partition was needed to make the journey less noisy. The bus operator would put a TV screen on the partition for customers to watch movies. Long-distance buses had better bodies, but that was it. They were lacking in terms of the engine and overall performance. There was no comfort.

Akash worked with a market research agency and the feedback he got was that 'if your buses are priced at ₹30 lakh, you will sell two buses; and with a ₹25 lakh pricing, you will sell six buses!' Akash junked the research. Here again was an intuitive marketer not going by standard research but his own field observations, which he believed were far superior to the research findings. He started meeting bus operators. They were not convinced about the service support from Volvo as the company didn't have manufacturing facilities in India then. Large fleet operators had their own service centres.

'Imagine a bus ride, then,' explains Akash. 'Luggage thrown on top, with tarpaulin on it; bags flung down upon arriving at the destination. A corporate executive travelling by bus then would probably be conscious about using his worst bag or suitcase for the journey as he wouldn't want his nice luggage to be damaged!'

This is where Volvo came in as a value proposition—it was not just based on technology but showcased how the technology was solving problems. It promised a comfortable ride and safe, secure, noiseless, air-conditioned travel, especially for long-distance travellers. Says Akash about a live demonstration they did:

> The Volvo bus had a rear engine, there was no noise, the driver sat low and there was no need for a partition. The driver would be able to sit in air-conditioned comfort for the first time. He, too, could enjoy the journey. The operator was unsure as he felt that the driver, sitting in his vest and lungi, would be embarrassing for the traveller. But here he was, in a smart uniform, acting like the coach captain!
>
> The bus operator couldn't believe that the power steering was so easy to handle. We demonstrated it by asking women to do the test drive. The operators were stunned. The drivers said it was easier than driving a car. It had to be! They had the 240-HP engine helping them!

The customer was naturally pleased as the new bus chassis allowed a luggage area where bags were securely kept, unlike on the bus's roof. Akash says, 'We didn't want openable windows, which otherwise would kill the concept. The only regulation was the driver door. That was allowed, unlike in other countries.' He continues:

> When we introduced the buses with a few operators, we immediately got customer feedback that felt fresh—they said there was no noise, no trucks honking, more leg space, the high torque of the engine giving them a smooth ride. When it was going at 100 kmph, the passengers never realized it. It saved many hours in the journey. Compared to normal buses,

the customer paid more and was happy to do so as they were getting tremendous value in return.

Our main USP was that we were able to get the government to change the bus length to 12 metres, which allowed space for the engine in the rear. We were able to create a forty-five-seater bus with more leg room than a thirty-seater, be it AC or non-AC.

Akash explains how the buses were being operated before Volvo came along to disrupt the market:

> For a bus operator, a luxury AC bus cost ₹15 to ₹25 lakh. Volvo cost ₹40 lakh plus. Our customer, that is the bus operator, complained he would not make money. But then he actually started charging a premium and made a lot of money as a result! We knew that our value proposition would work as we had introduced the buses with the end customer in mind. Unlike the market research report, which said there is no market, I knew that the market was huge—it just needed to be created. For us, technology was a key differentiator. And we made a huge difference to the traveller and the driver, and, in turn, to the bus operator, too, as his margins went up.

But how did they popularize such an expensive bus, we wondered.

Akash elaborates, 'We began with the south, followed by the west and north and then finally tackled the east. It is a word-of-mouth industry, and we allowed operators to talk to each other. Meanwhile, the customer had started demanding a "Volvo" experience as well. So that helped push sales.'

Volvo used mass media to full effect. We created thirty-second- and one-minute-long ad films and ran them in movie halls. There it was: a fancy bus going faster than a car. People couldn't believe it. They had never seen such a bus, and they were excited. Imagine a bus on the road overtaking you smoothly, noiselessly, while you believe you are zipping ahead in your car—that's the Volvo bus for you, without the black smoke!'

Customer insights are derived when a marketer observes the customer in action. Says Akash:

> In each bus we placed an intern who travelled with the customers to their destinations. At the end point, they would take feedback from the driver as well as the passengers. This feedback was so useful; we collected so much data. The customers had asked for simple things like a bottle of water, a blanket, earphones, and such. The driver and conductor were happy to wear good clothes, and proudly handed out baggage tags to the passengers, reminding them of air travel.
>
> We had asked the interns to call us if there was a problem with the bus. When the driver would call the Volvo service centre, he would be pleasantly surprised that his issue was already being taken care of, as the centre had been previously alerted by the intern before the driver could call.

Akash says that going slow helped. The company wanted to clearly demonstrate the efficiency of the better technology and how a value proposition would help the transporter. Volvo got a government agency to research the entire proposition, and they came out with a report on the operating performance of Volvo Buses. This report was then read by state corporations, who were convinced that Volvo offered something that they had not seen earlier. The faster buses, better fuel efficiency and the fact that the state corporations were losing business to private operators made them finally go for Volvo buses. Volvo had refused to discount the buses, but the corporations agreed to pay the premium price. Volvo thus got volumes in sales.

Akash recalls how a Volvo senior executive from Finland had ridiculed him when he had told him of his plan of selling 300 buses within a few years. The man had sniggered tauntingly, saying that Volvo sold that number in Finland. 'But in my third year, I had sold 303 buses and proven my senior wrong. They had not read the Indian market correctly. We are not a poor country. Indians are willing to pay if the value proposition is right. If there is value for money, people don't mind paying a higher amount. We had got the equation right,' Akash says proudly.

The Jawaharlal Nehru National Urban Renewal Mission (JNNURM) also gave the company a push. Volvo had already sold buses to the Bengaluru Metropolitan Transport Corporation and, by the time JNNURM came, Bangalore bought another 800. 'We supplied 2,000 of the 10,000 buses under JNNURM,' says Akash.

A marketer sometimes gets feedback in the most unexpected moments. Akash recalls sitting in a cafe in Whitefield, Bengaluru, when a customer walked up to him and thanked him for saving his time and, money. 'I travel daily from Koramangala to Whitefield, and thanks to the Volvo run by BMTC, I save time and money, and keep up my good health as I am not exposed to pollution while travelling around in air-conditioned comfort,' the customer said, offering to buy him a glass of wine as a token of thanks. Akash says, 'It is this kind of feedback that makes me feel like we have done a great job.'

We couldn't agree more. Volvo was not selling a product alone but a service that added value to the lives of people.

Soon, as expected, Volvo became associated with safe and comfortable air-conditioned travel, and spawned copycats who blatantly put the Volvo brand name and trademark on their buses. To ensure they stayed on the right side of the law, their signage would read, 'Like Volvo'. Akash found that there were 50,000 such buses in India but it made no sense running after them with legal cases. They had to deal with existing customers who had bought a few Volvo buses but were promoting many others in their fleet as 'Volvo'. 'You can fool the customer once but not each time. Soon, customers were discerning enough to find out if the ticket they had bought was for a genuine Volvo or not. They would look under the chassis to see if there was a leaf spring or air suspension, which identified it as a Volvo. Customers also checked if there were six bellows or four. Customers are not fools, and they would then argue and fight with the bus operator for having cheated them. And operators soon realized that they can't go on with the charade.'

Akash says with a smile, 'We knew we were selling to B2B customers but our business was B2C! Now, with the latest design, a tall boy image, even copying it is not easy.' He adds:

> There is a saying in marketing that 'Jo dikhta hai woh bikta hai'—what you see is what sells. But we proved it wrong. Superficial similarities between two products will go only so far. Finally, performance matters, and that is what will last. The Volvo brand is so strong that even state transport booking apps have a specific option for Volvo buses. We ride on technology. Eventually, better performance will prevail. A swanky body with a front engine will look good, but the customer experience won't be what a Volvo offers.

As we step out of our meeting with Akash, we are impressed by the story of how Volvo created a market when, seemingly, at first, it didn't look like it would exist. Indians are cost-conscious but it doesn't mean they will not pay for good performance and value. Vispy referred to a recent newspaper article about car sales in India which stated that SUVs were selling more than sedans. Indians are aspirational and want a better travel experience. And Volvo buses are just one way the traveller can be ensured comfortable long-distance travel. The recent popularity of Vande Bharat trains is another example of the customer being willing to pay a premium for comfort and speed. Volvo created a market and didn't fall for what market research was telling them. Most successful marketers are careful about the way they use data and how they process what others are telling them.

> *We can learn a lot from the Volvo story. In an aspirational economy, a good value proposition will work. What Volvo has demonstrated is that though Indians are traditionally cost-conscious, there is a growing segment that demands quality and is willing to pay for it. Today, with improved road infrastructure and people asking for a better travel experience, the luxury bus segment, especially for inter-city travel, is growing faster and larger. Volvo is best placed to take advantage of the transformation as luxury bus travel in India has become synonymous with brand Volvo.*
>
> *Volvo's buses in India were a game-changer, not only elevating the standards of bus travel but also demonstrating the potential of premium services in a cost-conscious market. Despite challenges, their success showcased the appetite for quality and comfort in public transportation.*

That 'Volvo' is now a generic word for comfortable and premium travel shows the extent to which the brand has become a part of the Indian consumer's psyche.

CONCLUSION

Creating a market for itself is, at times, like creating a blue ocean for the brand to swim freely in, without the danger of sharks. In the examples we discussed, the brand owner had the courage to create a blue ocean, thus reaching leadership levels. The space created by the brand will not remain uncluttered as competition will surely move in—once it sees the potential in the market created. But the first-mover advantage will stay. Provided, of course, the brand and its owner continue to remain agile and relevant.

We can look at some case studies from other countries to drive home this point. Marvel Entertainment was facing bankruptcy in the late 1990s, when it shifted from solely publishing comic books to creating its own movie production studio. By producing films featuring its comic characters, Marvel not only revitalized its brand but also redefined the superhero genre, leading to unprecedented success with the Marvel Cinematic Universe.

In a dying industry like that of circuses, Cirque du Soleil is an outlier. By blending circus arts with theatrical elements, Cirque du Soleil has crafted a unique form of entertainment that appeals to adults and corporate clients, differentiating itself from traditional circuses and creating a new market space. For decades, taxis were owned and operated by individuals or small companies. Uber disrupted the traditional industry by introducing a ride-hailing platform that connects drivers with passengers through a mobile app, creating a new market for on-demand transportation services. In a similar move, in the hospitality industry, Airbnb transformed the entire space by enabling homeowners to rent out their properties and, in the process, created a vast network of accommodations, offering travellers unique lodging experiences beyond what is available with traditional hotels.

By focusing on value innovation, creating an uncontested market space and solving unique customer problems, a brand can establish itself as a leader in a blue ocean market, minimizing competition while maximizing growth and profitability.

Creating a market is a sure but difficult path to tread. Most brands look for a gap in the existing product offerings and try to bring in a 'differentiated product', rather than creating something unique. This is where a marketer with conviction steps in, offering a solution to a problem and, in the process, establishes brand leadership.

PART 2

Creating a Need

There are needs and then there are wants. A consumer buys a product believing it will satisfy their needs. They desire the brand, ask for it by name, yet unknowingly, they chase the fulfilment of a deeper, more inherent need. This is why truly successful brands don't simply cater to wants; they dive into the core of human necessity, transforming needs into aspirational desires.

But in markets where needs are unstated or hidden, a shrewd marketer finds opportunity—a vast, unclaimed frontier waiting to be explored. Paras Pharma epitomized this strategy, crafting a portfolio of brands that anticipated and addressed these latent needs. Their success culminated in a monumental acquisition by Reckitt Benckiser. Yet, this story is less about the payoff and more about the mindset that made it possible.

Considered apocryphal, there is the tale of two shoe salesmen venturing into a market where no one wears shoes. One concludes, 'No one wears shoes—there's no market here.' The other exclaims, 'No one wears shoes—this market is untouched!' The difference lies in perception; for the astute marketer, an unfulfilled need is not a challenge—it's a gold mine.

The craft lies in recognizing this need, shaping it and then creating a brand that fills the void. When done masterfully, the result feels inevitable—even revolutionary. Think of Apple's iPod. No one imagined carrying thousands of songs in their pocket, but it reshaped music consumption overnight. Before that, Sony's Walkman introduced the world to personal audio. Kindle redefined how books were read and carried, revolutionizing publishing. These weren't just products—they were answers to needs no one had fully articulated.

However, the road to success is fraught with missteps. Misreading a need—or worse, inventing one without consumer backing—can lead to spectacular failures. Adman Subhash Kamath recounts a misstep from Parachute when they introduced a 'Lite' oil, assuming younger consumers would embrace a non-sticky option. The logic seemed sound: 'Non-sticky oil meets modern needs.' Yet, women rejected it outright. Why? They saw oiling as a laborious task, one that should ideally provide maximum benefit. The Lite oil felt weak, insubstantial—like water. It didn't penetrate the hair; it lingered uselessly on the surface.

As Subhash explains, 'It's a classic case of solving a need that exists only in the manufacturer's mind—not the consumer's.' In contrast, Bajaj Almond positioned its product as a nourishing oil with 'discovered' lightness—a subtle distinction that resonated deeply.

Another example highlights how even well-intentioned problem-solving can alienate loyal consumers. Subhash shares the story of Horlicks, where the sediment left at the bottom of the glass was perceived as a flaw by some. Another brand, Viva, attempted to capitalize on this by launching an instant-dissolve variant. Yet, Horlicks loyalists cherished the sediment, seeing it as proof of the product's richness—'the extra goodness', they called it, savouring it slowly after the milk was drained. The supposed flaw was, in fact, part of the magic. Most marketers fail not because of lack of effort but because they cannot uncover the latent, unspoken needs of their audience. They miss the subtle, emotional truths that define consumer behaviour.

Vispy, with his experience at Ormax Consultants, calls this 'the penny-dropping moment'—the instant when a brand connects with a latent need so perfectly that the consumer's response is an emotional *aha*! These moments are rare, precious and transformative. Reflecting on his years of experience, Vispy fondly recalls collaborating with Darshan bhai, as Darshan Patel, the founder of Paras Pharma, is called, whom he describes as one of the most intuitive marketers he's ever worked with.

Brands that succeed in these moments don't merely sell products—they change lives. They tap into desires consumers didn't know they had, turning silent longings into unforgettable experiences. And for those who master this art, the reward is not just success but a legacy.

12

ITCH GUARD AND RING GUARD: SOLVING AN ITCHY PROBLEM

Let us turn to a problem millions face but are shy to admit to in public. And if it occurs in places which one can't talk about openly, it becomes a huge problem.

When it comes to ringworm, people have been troubled for years. It is not something that goes away easily. The ringworm isn't a worm. It's a skin infection that's caused by mould-like fungi that live in the dead tissues of your skin, hair and nails. You can get ringworm in any of these places—and on your scalp. When you get it between your toes, it's what people call athlete's foot. Paras Pharma made a business out of it by focusing on the problem with clear communication. Let us look at how the company launched brands in this area and created leaders.

Itch Guard and Ring Guard are brands created out of a latent need—one that always existed for the consumer but had neither been articulated in the form of a solution nor been explicitly demanded. There were some brands trying to solve the problem, but it was the clear communication from Paras Pharma which made it a winner.

There is a constant itch afflicting many consumers in tropical India, especially in the humid regions of the country. It is often in uncomfortable areas, where one does not want to publicly acknowledge the itch but is desperate to scratch and wishes that it would just go away. (In the Western world, the itch in the groin area is referred to colloquially as a 'jock itch'.)

Paras Pharma came out with Itch Guard—the name distinctly telling customers what the solution to their problem was—and it became a bestseller overnight. The image of itchy bacteria found resonance with the consumer. It was similar to the itchy bug used for Vicks Cough Drops. In an advertisement for Itch Guard, a security chief is shown inspecting his gang of personnel in uniform; instead of his pants, however, he is wearing a towel. In the next shot a man dressed in formals from head to waist, but with a towel wrapped around his hips, walks in a crowd. In yet another shot, a group of men hanging from a local train sport towels instead of pants. In another, a man with a towel in place of trousers is out on a date. The song in the background with the words 'Jaane de, jaane de, mausam ko jaane de, hawa aane de. Dekhti hai duniya toh dekhne de, hawa aane de.' In the next shot, a rather irritated animated man wearing pants is shown running and sweating at the same time and the voiceover, referring to the towel-clad men, says, 'Kaash aap aisa kar paate.' The explanation follows through the voiceover, 'Active zindagi, yeh mausam, aur tang kapde ... toh paseene waali khujli hona aam baat hain. Aise mein lagaye Itch Guard.' In the next shot, an engineer, atop a building, throws his towel away, suggesting that now he can wear his trousers and still be comfortable.

Darshan Patel explains:

> Tight clothing in hot and humid weather makes us feel uncomfortable and sweaty. The insight from our research

> was that after coming back home, people like to wrap a towel around themselves, having removed their trousers, as they feel free from the discomfort of wearing trousers all day. We wanted to bring in the 'I wish I could wear a towel outside' feeling through the ad. We have adapted to Western styles of clothing in the hot and humid climate of India. This causes a lot of sweat and itching problems. Anti-itching creams were not used widely by people because of the common misconception that they are for more severe problems.

Says Vispy, talking about the ads which show different and often humorous situations:

> The brand became an instant success. But success had its fair share of problems as well. The consumer research we carried out showed that Itch Guard was perceived as a brand for 'serious' itches. That meant there was restricted usage of the product. And there was a concern that Itch Guard may be perceived as providing relief for itches only in the groin area. Hence, the brand decided to reposition and separate campaigns were run for broadening the usage and also to make the brand appealing to sufferers of a non-serious itch. Even the brand name, with the 'itch' depicted like thorns, helped communicate instantly the reason why it existed. It was clear to the customer.

Vispy explains how the brand communication was created to include many 'fence-sitters'. Research showed that Itch Guard already had a loyal customer base, with regular communications going on for several years. The trick, therefore, was to target the non-users or those who felt embarrassed to use Itch Guard. The existing idea—of getting caught while scratching, which causes embarrassment both to oneself and one's significant other—came under the scanner. All communication over the years on this platform had exhausted its appeal. While it did get them trials and loyalists thereafter, it was not working on the fence-sitters, who perceived Itch Guard as a serious remedy for a serious problem not suffered by them. Ironically, a product that prevented embarrassment actually became an embarrassing product to ask for at the counter. That is where a different set of commercials were worked upon following a consumer study.

Vispy found from his research that there was a need to redefine the 'khujli', the itch—by giving it a newer, more universally acceptable casualness. 'This had to be lifestyle-related and not a physiological condition,' he says.

It was clear that if Itch Guard was to acquire a desirable persona, it would automatically transcend any condition-related imagery and become acceptable to non-users too.

In the later Itch Guard ads, we find colloquial expressions people use to talk to each other about while getting started on any activity, 'Chal ho ja shuru.' Since highly active people are seen as achievers, they would colloquially be addressed as 'guru'. Hence, the tie-up: 'Guru, ho ja shuru.' And the counter, 'Guru, phir se ho ja shuru.'

In another series of ads, through a catchy phrase like 'Haath hai yahaan' and the question, 'Haath hai kahaan?' the commercial conveys that using Itch Guard will ensure freedom from itching, thus allowing the freedom to use your hands for various other activities.

Vispy further elaborates:

> Itch Guard has successfully created a category for itself. For the customers, the brand has made their lives a lot easier. It also removed the taboo surrounding this problem. One of the successes of the brand was that it was able to understand that itch-related problems are more a lifestyle issue than a hygiene issue. This insight has helped the brand communicate with the customer in a more refined manner.

This positioning has also helped customers purchase this brand without any embarrassment.

Itch Guard is a classic marketing story where a brand identifies a problem and successfully solves it. By addressing a significant consumer need with a well-crafted product and marketing strategy, Itch Guard became a trusted brand in the Indian pharmaceutical and personal care market. The brand also reminds marketers that even in this clutter, it is possible to come up with successful brands if you listen to the customer.

'Itch Guard really took off once we communicated the problem and its solution; and it remains a leader,' says Darshan bhai.

Like the itchy bacteria causing irritation, ringworm was another problem millions in India faced. However, the communication was not as straightforward as most people didn't want to talk about the issue publicly—as it was perceived as an embarrassing problem.

Ring Guard decided to approach this matter in a direct way. There was no confusion, and it told the consumer what it stood for. In the case of ringworm, the problem was different from sweat-related itching as most consumers would not want to admit that they had ringworm. Research showed that customers were not comfortable talking about it to friends but were fine disclosing it to a chemist. When it came to ringworm, the chemist was a big influencer, and Ring Guard ensured that the chemist was well aware of the brand. The solution was thus not as easy as Itch Guard. There were other products in the market already, like BTEX, Saibol, Zalim Lotion and such, but they all burnt the skin, and even left one with a stinging feeling and a black patch, which was ugly. Thus, while these remedies were popular in different local markets, there was clearly a gap to address.

Research showed that customers were also advised that local remedies like garlic juice, kerosene, lime and neem leaves could be rubbed on the affected area for relief. People were trying all kinds of things to get rid of their 'daad, khaaj, khujli', as it was referred to in Hindi.

Consumer research by Vispy and team highlighted the common belief in people that scratching the affected area would bring the worms to the surface and the 'daad' would start all over again. The overall expectation was that symptomatic relief was extremely important. They just wanted to get rid of the scratchy feeling.

Daad, khaj and khujli were considered problems for which a long-term solution had not been found. While many local products offered relief, the problem tended to resurface soon. Research also showed that an ointment was considered better than a lotion, which would run off; and also that a lotion was difficult to apply in the infected area and was messier. It was also found that the customer wanted the 'maddening scratching' to stop immediately. They wanted to be able to return to normalcy in their work and personal lives, and this was considered very important. Additionally, the customer didn't want any trace of the 'daad' left behind. They all expected that there would either be a white patch, a black patch or thick skin left behind once the treatment ran its course. They feared that the discoloration would take a long time to go away, and that till it did, they were not fully healed. Quite surprisingly, the burning feeling of using some of the other brands was considered a double-barrelled issue as the customer was unsure whether the burning was good or bad.

The research brought out the fact that the brand could take the position as the only solution specifically for ringworm. BTEX and salical creams were sold in dabbis, which were considered cumbersome to open, and there was also the fear that the tin could rust. The Ring Guard tube was thus seen as a better idea. It could be applied by anybody without staining their fingers. The red-coloured pack also stood out clearly against the blue and white of BTEX and the yellow and red of salical creams.

Quite naturally, the product couldn't be advertised the way Itch Guard was, which used humour and daily situations. The brand was sold through chemists extensively and soon occupied the top position as a cure for ringworm infection. Once again, a direct approach was preferred, and the brand became a leader in no time. Ring Guard and Itch Guard are clear examples of a solution for a need which had never been explicitly expressed.

> *By addressing a common yet underserved medical need with targeted marketing, accessible pricing and effective distribution by pharmacists, Ring Guard carved out a strong niche in the market, becoming a go-to solution for fungal infections in India.*

There are many problems like itching due to sweat, which are left unaddressed for lack of a specific solution. As we saw, Darshan Patel and his team not only addressed the gap but created brands which continue to be leaders till today.

13

LIVON: TACKLING A KNOTTY PROBLEM

In India, as is the case the world over, women tend to fret about their hair. The climate, the water and the pollution all come together to make women feel as though they will never be rid of the frizz. And it tends to get worse after a wash, despite using shampoo.

The problem of hair frizz had been left unaddressed ever since shampoos were introduced in India. It was a problem screaming to be tackled, with no one giving it a serious thought. A sharp marketing mind is always looking for such opportunities, and Paras Pharma, once again, was not going to let the opportunity pass. 'I work for one thing: a differentiated product,' says Darshan Patel, founder, Paras Pharma, while conceding that the approach has its pitfalls. 'It is a dangerous proposition because if no such product exists in the market, the consumers might reject it. But I feel it is better to die differentiating than creating something that is already there.'

Vispy knows this—he has worked with Darshan bhai for decades. He explains, 'Darshan bhai's insights and clarity of thought are outstanding. While MNCs create a product and then brand it, Darshan bhai creates a brand, identifying the need gap in the market, and then builds a product around it.'

Let us look at the story of Livon. It is another example of a need badly felt but with no solution in sight—in this case, of hair frizz occurring, especially after a shampoo wash. This was a huge problem for women in India. This is where Paras Pharma's Livon captured the market. Today, there is no brand, literally, which competes in that space with Livon.

'As long as we have hair to wash, there have been shampoos—for thousands of years,' says Prof. Dhananjay Sane, a sociology professor. We went out on a market visit to understand the category. Vispy had studied the brand from a research perspective, but we felt it was important to get a first-hand impression for the purpose of our story.

Curious to know more, we went to a chemist's shop. 'Did you know that shampooing was first invented in India?' asked Ramesh, the shopkeeper. He has a postgraduate degree in pharmacy and knows a thing or two about chemicals. We listen to him with curiosity. He told us:

> 'Shampoo' is derived from the Hindi word 'champu', which, in turn, evolved from the Sanskrit word 'chapyathi', which essentially means 'to massage or press'. The practice of using shampoo dates back to 1500 CE, or maybe even before, when a concoction of boiled reetha [soap berries], amla [gooseberry], hibiscus, shikakai [acacia] and other hair-friendly herbs was made and used on the scalp to cleanse the tresses.
>
> In many households across India, grandmothers still follow this practice of drying certain leaves and flowers and making a paste from it. If my nonagenarian grandmother had her way, she would still be making her own shampoo powder.

I agree. I am aware of shikakai as I have used it in my childhood. Ramesh continues by telling us the story of Sake Dean Mahomed, born in 1759 in Patna, who belonged to the barber community:

> The young lad had grown up learning techniques for making herbal potions and soaps. Along the way, he also learnt the art of giving people a champi (head massage).
>
> At the age of eleven, Mahomed joined the East India Company army and rose to the rank of captain. He fought in a number of campaigns until 1782, when he resigned from the army. He arrived in Britain two years later. It was in Brighton that he opened a spa, which he called Mahomed's Baths, where he offered head-massage treatments to his clients.
>
> He was so well-known for his head massages that he was soon made King George IV's and King William IV's personal 'shampoo surgeon'. His popularity was so staggering that hospitals would even refer patients to him, earning him the moniker 'Dr Brighton'. He went on to publish a book called *Shampooing, or Benefits Resulting from the Use of Indian Medicated Vapour Bath.*

Ramesh tells us that it was only much later in the 1900s that the meaning of shampoo shifted from being a mere massage to an application of another substance to the hair to cleanse it.

As we were looking at the rows of shampoo bottles displayed in Ramesh's shop, he said, 'We have come a long way from Sake Dean Mahomed's invention. Today, there are all kinds of shampoos available in the market, in different permutations and combinations for different needs—for dry hair, coloured hair and even baby hair.'

We nod. Some of us use baby shampoo after a swim every day as it is gentle on the hair. We know many sportspersons who do that too. Johnson's Baby Shampoo increased its market share in the US by targeting sportspersons. It was shown as effective in removing sweat and residue. Athletes often deal with sweat build-up, chlorine build-up (for swimmers) and residue from helmets or protective gear. Baby shampoo was marketed as being effective for gentle cleansing without stripping away the natural oils.

We ponder on what exactly hair is, and a trichologist in Mumbai tells us:

> Hair has three main components. It is made of protein called keratin, natural oils that keep hair flexible and water. The outside part, the part we see, is the cuticle and is made of five to ten overlapping layers of protein. The middle section is the cortex, which gives the hair strength and prevents it from breaking, and the centre is an empty zone or medulla, which helps insulate the hair.

Ramesh added to the trichologist's explanation and told us:

> When it comes to hair products, the most important part is the cuticle. When the layers of protein lie smoothly against each other, it looks shiny and smooth. Daily washing and brushing make the cuticle stand up straight, making it frizzy and creating split ends.

Adds a marketing veteran who has worked for companies like Hindustan Unilever and Procter & Gamble:

> The world began to see shampoo in its modern form with Drene Shampoo. Thus began our collective love affair with shampoo and the sensation of lather on our heads. As with many products marketed to both professionals and consumers, shampoo became increasingly specialized, to address a number of desires and conditions—thin, thick, curly, dry, oily, blonde, coloured, ethnic, young and old hair—and to sell as much of it as possible. And for every shampoo, there is a companion: the conditioner.

This is where Livon from Paras Pharma saw an opportunity. They wanted to fulfil a specific need—that of making hair easy to brush after using shampoo.

Market research by Vispy and team showed that shampoo is a functional product which cleans hair well. It also works to remove dandruff. But there was a larger question of what women really wanted. The insights team looked at addressing the question: What keeps a woman awake at night? Research showed that one of the biggest problems in a woman's life is hair fall. Hair, for women, is considered one of the most attractive beauty attributes. It is even more important than skin. For a woman, losing hair is akin to a disaster.

Now that research showed that hair fall was a concern for woman, the question was: How does one address the same? The answers ranged from nothing could be done about it to a lack of vitamins to worry and stress and more. The Livon research team tried to understand how a woman knew whether she had lost hair. What they found was that this realization comes when she sees hair on her pillow in the morning, when combing her hair after a bath or clogging the bathroom drain. Women panic when they see drastic hair loss and start looking for magic remedies. Vispy details the research:

> The issue was whether the woman was losing hair from her roots or was it something else. The hair on the pillow is from the roots, but when she combs it, the hair she sees on her comb is due to the physical act of hair breaking. That happens mainly when she takes a shampoo bath. Her hair knots up and she loses a lot of hair, which then gets entangled in her comb. The comb she uses leads to breakage. She sees this as hair loss but does not know the solution to it.

The Livon team realized that not only was this an opportunity to solve a problem but that this space was unoccupied as well. It was a need nobody had addressed despite being visible to everyone. Here was a chance for them to get first-mover advantage.

What was needed was a detangler. The word 'serum' was not used much then. Livon was, in fact, a serum which could solve the problem of frizzy and tangled hair. It would detangle the hair and not cause hair loss.

Once again, the approach of using a simple but effective brand name was employed. Livon was clear in its name: 'Leave it on' and the hair would not break!

Despite some initial hiccups, the brand soon became popular. Their extensive and accurate communication made a difference.

A consumer needed just a few drops of Livon to make their hair smooth and free from breakage.

Check out the old advertisements of Livon. A girl with frizzy hair is wondering how she can attend a party that she has just come to hear of. She hurries to set up a salon appointment at home, as the voiceover reminds viewers that it's impossible to enjoy home service all the time. The solution? Just wet your hair and apply a few drops of Livon. The catchline 'Salon nahi, Livon' perfectly sums up the product and how it can be used.

Most battles are fought in the shelf space. For Livon, it was another challenge as it was a product category which didn't exist. It is neither a shampoo nor a hair oil. Soon, retailers realized that selling it along with a bottle of shampoo made sense as the customer was using Livon to solve a problem she had always faced.

Another element to consider was the pricing of the product. Livon was Paras Pharma's most expensive product. The question was whether such a costly product would be accepted by the market. The research team found that in the customer's mind the price of a product was relative to the value offered, and that it was not an absolute concept. If the customer felt the product was offering the right value, she was willing to pay for it. The ads don't have to quote the exact prices, but the product features make it clear that while it is 'expensive', compared to some other products, it was worth it. When

Livon compares itself to a home salon, it is evident that it would be priced much more than a shampoo or a bottle of regular hair oil. When Darshan Patel launched Livon, it was priced at ₹140 for a small 50 ml bottle. 'It was the first time I had sold something at that price point, and it worked. The lesson was that if we see a need gap, we must fill it with the right product—and the consumer will pay,' he says. Vispy explains:

> The market research showed that the user liked the product and was convinced that it was not oil, as it didn't leave any stains on the hand. They liked that it was chemical-free and thus not harsh, as there was no colour [the serum was almost transparent], and that there was no smell. All the attributes of the product had been perceived well by the customer.

While the initial campaign was a hit, consumer research showed that everyone had overwhelmingly said that Livon left hair silky and smooth but that the brand had missed the detangler part being expressly mentioned in the ad. This was taken into account and soon new communication ensured that the customer got the sequence right: Washing hair left knots, which lead to breakage when the hair was brushed. But if one applied Livon, it helped remove the knots, which made detangling easier, leading to decreased hair loss and smoother hair.

Once again, consumer insights had ensured that the advertising and communication clearly spoke of the long-term sustainability of the brand.

Marico launched a product called Silk-N-Shine to compete with Livon, but it looked like a shampoo and talked of silky, long hair and other attributes which are already present in a shampoo. It never succeeded despite being priced much lower than Livon. (Later, in 2012, Marico bought a few of Paras Pharma brands like Livon, which had been earlier bought by Reckitt Benckiser.)

We go back to Ramesh to study a few bottles of conditioner. We are surprised by his response:

> In India, conditioner, as a product, is a disaster because nobody uses it. Conditioner is the fancy relative of the shampoo that

> only people in the West use. Indians are far more practical—especially now that most shampoos have conditioners built into it. Conditioners never took off in India. People still don't know how to use a conditioner. Conditioner removes the static electricity in hair, which is good, but Livon not only removes static electricity, it also prevents hair from tangling.

We ask Ramesh whether any other brand like Livon sells. He shakes his head. 'There is no other,' he admits.

Livon is a classic example of first identifying a need which has always existed and then finding a solution for it. It continues to be a brand leader even today.

Livon was one of the first brands in India to introduce hair serum as a mainstream product. It solved common hair issues like frizz, tangles and dullness, creating a new category in the haircare market. The brand positioned itself as a quick solution for achieving manageable, salon-like hair. The target audience was clear: Livon focused on young, modern women looking for quick and effective hair solutions, appealing to their busy lifestyles and desire for effortless beauty. Memorable campaigns like 'Get Salon-Finish Hair' resonated with the consumers. Showing clear before and after shots demonstrated the product's efficacy as well.

Livon successfully addressed all the elements of the brand—the name, the small and conveniently sized bottle, the extensive and effective communication strategy and the price point.

14

CEASEFIRE: OWN SOMETHING YOU WILL HOPEFULLY NEVER NEED

There are needs far more primal and urgent than frizzy hair—like the fear of losing a loved one to a fire at home. Surprisingly, no one had addressed this need until a determined marketer stepped in to communicate both the urgency and the solution convincingly.

Ceasefire captured the market's imagination from day one, becoming the default name for home fire safety. Yet, the company lost focus, diverting efforts to unrelated brands, and its dominance faded.

The Ceasefire story highlights a unique challenge: Even when customers are fully aware of a life-threatening risk like fire, behavioural inertia often prevents them from acting. The product's obvious value proposition wasn't enough. For a brand to succeed, it needed to address this hesitation and inspire proactive adoption.

At its launch, Ceasefire brilliantly combined consumer insight with product innovation and clear communication, tapping into an unmet need with undeniable relevance. The result? A product that resonated instantly, proving that with the right understanding of consumer behaviour, even uncharted categories can turn into overnight successes—if only focus and commitment endure.

Real Value Appliances, owned by Pheroze Engineer, started operations in 1989, bringing to the country a new concept—a domestic fire extinguisher. Fire extinguishers were not uncommon for Indian consumers. They saw them in large malls, offices, buildings and theatres—all public places. But a domestic fire extinguisher was unique. Indian consumers had never thought of having one in their homes. It was this uncanny fact that made Engineer design something for home use.

The product made perfect sense in the Indian market (in fact, every single market). Our households deal with fire all the time—be it for cooking or religious rituals—and the risk of catching fire very much exists. Hence, a marketing mind could easily see the prospect of cashing in on that need. And thus, Ceasefire was born.

The product was compact, unique, had a catchy name, looked good and boasted that it could extinguish all sorts of fires. Ceasefire was a Halon 1211–based fire extinguisher that was very compact, handy and easy to use, thus requiring minimal effort. Much more than the efficacy of use, it gave a certain peace of mind to the Indian consumer.

The product was well received in the market. The ads focused on building within the consumer a fear of a possible fire accident at home. The ads were backed by a sales campaign. The company focused on direct marketing to promote the product. Since this fear is so basic to the human psyche, the product's success was imminent. The product was priced at a premium, but the customers never complained.

Much like insurance, fire extinguishers are the kind of product where the customers are not unhappy if it is not being used. Hence, the success lay in stoking consumers' fears.

'A good advertisement is one that opens the door,' says ad guru Bharat Dabholkar. Adds Vispy, 'It is the "aha!" moment. The consumer gives permission to the marketer to talk about her emotions.' The positioning insight comes when marketers use this opportunity to talk directly to the consumer, establishing a chord of sympathy.

Vispy and his team have done a lot of research on fear and the consumer's response to it. It is an emotion which is not easy to ride on, though it looks like it is a simple one used to target the customer. He says, 'Research showed that the customer believed and intellectually agreed about the occurrence of fire but there was no incident in his life to relate to. It is like, "Accidents don't happen to me, so why should I wear a helmet?"'

The male ego is threatened. This is where the research team came up with a brilliant communication. The idea was to scare the husband with the thought that if a fire took place at home and his wife screamed, would he be able to hear it? The ad shows a pregnant woman leafing through a photo album at home, as she sits on her sofa in the drawing room. It is a pleasant day outside. The husband is busy in the office. As she goes into the kitchen, her pallu catches fire. The husband is oblivious to what is happening at home, as he busy doing his office work. There is laughter and chatter around him. Quite clearly, he cannot hear his wife's screams. Says Bharat:

> The ad clearly shows how vulnerability increases with distance. And urgency multiplies manifold. The communication was bang on. It got the husband to react. A small Ceasefire extinguisher would have done the job and saved the day. He doesn't hesitate to buy the product when the Ceasefire sales executive visits him the next day.

Ad man Subhash Kamath further adds:

> One of the insights was that a consumer would think, 'Such a big fire and such a small extinguisher.' So what they actually did was that they took a large table and set it on fire, and then they used the extinguisher on it successfully. It told the customer about the effectiveness of the product. The other insight was about the reluctance to buy and, hence, the ad showed that for the price of a cup of tea, you could protect your office from fire.

We ask Subhash whether, in the case of Ceasefire, it was a subtle balance between inducing fear and tapping into a customer's logic? He explains:

> Both. There were multiple tasks. One, we had to prove the product's efficacy with demonstrations. Second, we had to break the thinking, the mindset, that fires don't happen in general and to me in particular. We had to show that it could happen to anybody, so don't think that it can't happen to you. It can happen to you when you are least expecting it. So that was one part of the communication. To the businesses, we had to explain that the cost of fireproofing offices was less than a cup of tea. Then we had to work on education. For fire extinguishers, most instructions are in English. But most of the workers can't read English. Let us say there was a fire in the godown at night, and the instructions were in English. We used this scenario to tell the customer that your workers may not be able to read English. The customer was an MNC. We told the senior executives, 'See, these are things that these guys can't use, and you will lose millions if a fire breaks out.'
>
> We also had to educate people about the different types of fires. For instance, in the case of an electrical fire, you cannot throw water on it. There were thus multiple levels of

communication because it was all about inducing behaviour change.

Adds a marketing veteran, 'Ceasefire was a product that had understood a need which always existed and created a sense of urgency to buy it. It is unfortunate the company's successful run did not continue—it later diversified into vacuum cleaners and such, and lost its way.'

But the idea that a dormant product need could be brought to the fore was clearly demonstrated by Ceasefire. It was a brand that lost its life because of factors outside its control. But surprisingly, no other brand has come forward to take its position. The product category that was created by Ceasefire is still empty. Maybe the category does not appeal to other marketers. But there is always potential, as the fear remains.

There are clear takeaways from the Ceasefire story. The brand was a tremendous success, which unfortunately, for reasons outside the scope of this book, didn't allow it to maintain its leadership position.

Ceasefire introduced innovative and easy-to-use fire extinguishers and other fire-safety solutions, making fire protection accessible to homes, offices and small businesses, and not just industrial spaces. Their extinguishers were designed to tackle multiple types of fires (electrical, oil, wood, etc.), which simplified decision-making for consumers. Ceasefire focused on educating individuals and organizations about the importance of fire safety through campaigns, workshops and training programmes.

By highlighting the risks of fire accidents and the importance of preparedness, it created demand for their products. 'Ceasefire—because fire waits for no one' resonated with customers and emphasized urgency.

15

KRACK CREAM: MENDING CRACKED HEELS

If a marketer is alert and looking for a gap, he or she will surely find many. Like Ceasefire, which was all about riding on a need which was real, there are many problems which continue to remain unaddressed while waiting for a marketer to come along and bridge the gap.

Let us turn to one such story of an unfulfilled need.

Cracked heels. They are a classic case of a felt need, with no specific solutions yet. The genius of Paras Pharma was in not only identifying the need but emerging with a specific solution to address it, thus allowing the brand to hold a very strong position in the market. The challenge in launching such products is that, oftentimes, the customer is immune to their problem. They need to be awakened and made aware of it. But once the brand resonates with the unstated need, it becomes a leader.

This is the story of Krack Cream.

According to Vispy, who worked with Darshan Patel, the founder of Paras Pharma, on the research: 'At times, the problem is not just obvious—it is so common that it is not even considered a problem that needs to be solved.'

Cracked heels fell in this category. And this is where Paras Pharma stepped in with Krack Cream, which did exactly what its name suggested—mending cracked heels.

Simplistic as it sounds, there was no product specifically targeting a problems that millions of customers, especially women in India, faced. Those with cracked heels faced not just acute pain but also embarrassment.

When a problem is universal, it is often ignored and accepted as reality. 'The best place to hide something is in plain sight,' goes an old saying.

On a sweltering June afternoon in 1992, Darshan Patel sat in a bustling Mumbai suburban railway station. The rains had ceased, but the air remained heavy and humid. As thousands of commuters rushed past, Darshan bhai sat still. Watching. Observing. His focus wasn't on their faces or their hurried movements. He was staring at their feet.

Women's feet.

He noticed the same thing, again and again—cracked heels. Women wore chappals and sandals, their feet exposed to relentless heat, dust and hard surfaces. In contrast, men's shoes protected their heels—shielding them from the elements, keeping their skin soft and supple. Women, barefoot at home, vulnerable outside, bore the brunt of a problem that no one had truly perceived. Cracked heels weren't just unsightly. When the cracks deepened, they became painful—so painful that even walking was agony. Sarees caught in those fissures amplified the discomfort.

Darshan Patel saw what no one else had: a persistent, ignored problem. A need hiding in plain sight.

His next step was clear. Research. Market surveys led by Vispy and his team uncovered a startling truth—there was no dedicated solution for cracked heels. Women were resigned to temporary fixes: oils, Vaseline, home remedies. They had settled for relief that didn't last because no one had bothered to get to the root of the issue. Housewives, working women and domestic helpers alike shared the same complaint—the same pain.

This was more than a market gap, it was an unspoken cry for help. Thus, Krack Cream was born. It was not a generic moisturizer. Not a fleeting solution. It was a product designed specifically for cracked heels—a problem so obvious, yet so overlooked. Darshan Patel didn't just create a cream, he gave voice to a silent need, turning an invisible struggle into a focused solution.

For the first time, women didn't have to live with the pain. Krack Cream didn't just soothe cracked heels—it healed them.

Says Darshan Patel, 'No matter if your brand is new or old, you will find your path only through customer observation and research.' As it with most other products from Paras Pharma's stable, the name was simple, direct and communicated what it was meant to be used for—cracks in the feet! There was no fancy, complicated or subtle messaging in the ads.

The product was an instant success. Brilliance is often born from simplicity. And Krack Cream continues to be a leader even thirty years later.

As with other products, the communication strategy was based on extensive market studies, talking to customers and understanding their problems.

If you check out the old advertisements of Krack Cream, you will see how the problems faced by the women are addressed. In one ad, a lady, while showing off her expensive branded handbags and shoes, is suddenly embarrassed when her friends who, while admiring her shoes, notice her cracked heels. She is very reluctant to show her feet, and the friends taunt her saying, 'Dikhao, dikhao!' This ad was a result of the research, which showed that women considered cracked heels acutely embarrassing—regardless of their physical beauty and the nice clothes they wear. They felt all their beauty was nullified with cracked heels.

In another humorous ad, the police are trying to find a suspect, who would possibly have muddy feet. When asked to show their feet, one of the house members, a lady, hesitates, thus placing suspicion on herself. It is later clarified that she was hesitant to show her cracked heels, and everyone laughs at her. Striking the right chord with the customer's emotions is a sure way to make a brand successful.

Then there is the ad showing how a mother is reminded to take care of herself by using Krack Cream when her daughter is not around. We see a mother coming back home after seeing off her daughter. She notices packs of Krack Cream kept in several places with a note that says, 'Ma, bhoolna nahi.'

In yet another ad, the husband, who apparently doesn't seem to be bothered about his wife's cracked heels, makes a turnaround and hands her a pack of Krack Cream, though he is in a hurry to leave for work. In one more ad, the wife's beautiful face reminds the husband of a 'rani', in contrast to her cracked heels that make her look like a 'naukrani' or domestic helper. The ad is hard-hitting, true to emotions and instantly makes a connection with the consumer!

Then we see in another ad how a blindfolded boyfriend is happily visualizing the soft feather-like touch of his girlfriend's skin; but the moment she rubs her heels against his legs he imagines a prickly cactus!

'Krack Cream is about love and care' was the message. Research showed that while the customer was happy to find a solution, the messaging of love and care sealed the relationship.

As is the case with products launched from Paras Pharma's stable, the packaging is not unique. Rather, it is quite ordinary, with the words 'Krack Cream' written prominently inside an image of a foot. The relentless communication ensured that it resonated with the customer, her emotions, and it made her feel that there was now a product which not only spoke to her but also recognized her problems. Krack Cream addressed her needs, which always existed but had never been given importance. A product becomes a leader when the customer realizes that the brand is speaking her language. And 'understands' her.

Krack Cream solved a simple, universal problem—one which had been around forever but which no one had cared to acknowledge or find a solution for. No wonder, then, that it commands a whopping 80 per cent of the market share.[1]

There are many learnings from the story of Krack Cream. By focusing on a specific need, Krack Cream carved out a niche for itself in the competitive skincare market. This targeted positioning helped the brand stand out in a crowded market of general skincare products. The brand effectively positioned itself as a remedy for an uncomfortable yet common problem. Its marketing highlighted both the discomfort caused by cracked feet and the relief that Krack Cream provided.

Advertisements often focused on the real-life problem of cracked heels and the solution offered by the product, using relatable scenarios that resonated with consumers. Memorable, simple and relatable taglines such as 'Goodbye cracked heels' made the product easy to remember and identified it directly with the solution to footcare issues.

Darshan Patel and his team acted on their observations, which resulted in blockbuster success. Krack Cream revolutionized footcare in India with its effective, affordable and widely trusted healing formula.

---

1. 'Brinton cracks strategic alliance with Scholl Wellness Company', *Business Standard*, 2 March 2022, https://www.business-standard. com/ content/press-releases-ani/brinton-cracks-strategic-alliance-with-scholl-wellness-company-122030200393_1.html, accessed on 3 April 2025.

CONCLUSION

True innovation doesn't just answer existing questions. It dares to ask the ones no one has thought of yet. It's not about simply filling gaps but about uncovering the unseen, unspoken and unmet desires of consumers before they can even realize they exist. The most transformative products don't just offer solutions, they create entirely new expectations.

When smartphones emerged, they weren't merely a better version of mobile phones—they shattered conventional thinking. A device that combined calling, photography, navigation and entertainment wasn't something consumers had explicitly demanded. Yet when it arrived, it became indispensable. Today, we don't just use our phones, we live through them. Similarly, before Netflix, Prime Video and Spotify, people were content with scheduled programming and physical media. They didn't explicitly ask for the ability to stream anything, anywhere, anytime. But once that possibility was introduced, it didn't just become popular—it became the new standard.

Latent needs are the whispers of the future: subtle, unexpressed, yet immensely powerful. The greatest innovations aren't just about addressing current consumer problems, they're about staying ahead of the curve—seeing not just what people want now, but what they will need before they even know it themselves. The rise of ten-minute delivery services like Zepto and Blinkit is a testament to this tendency. A few years ago, no one was impatient for groceries to arrive in minutes. But now? We need our groceries delivered as soon as possible and the alternative seems unacceptable. This is the power of foresight—reshaping behaviour, redefining convenience and setting new benchmarks for what is possible.

But even the most groundbreaking innovation is meaningless without the right positioning. The price is never just about the cost—it's about value. Consumers don't judge a product by its price tag alone, but by the impact it delivers. The most successful brands don't hesitate to price their products higher when they provide a superior experience. They don't wait for consumers to recognize their worth—they communicate it with clarity and conviction. Real and consistent messaging is what elevates a brand from being just another option to being the only choice.

The companies that truly succeed don't just react to market trends, they define them. They identify gaps, not by following demand, but by shaping it. They don't just create products, they craft experiences, shift perceptions and build deep emotional connections. They challenge the status quo, disrupt entire industries and, in doing so, leave an indelible mark on the world.

At the heart of every iconic brand lies a simple truth: they have the ability to see what others don't, the courage to believe in something before the world does and the tenacity to turn an idea into a movement. The future belongs to those who don't just meet needs—but create them.

PART 3

Creating Brands from Commodities

Many of today's iconic brands have risen from the ashes of heavily commoditized industries—industries so saturated that the product itself often defines the category. Names like Band-Aid, Xerox and Dalda are no longer just brands; they've become cultural shorthand for the commodities they represent. Still, even these giants must constantly innovate to keep their edge and stand out on increasingly crowded shelves.

The transformation of a commodity into a brand is no small feat. It demands a deep, almost intimate, understanding of consumer needs and desires. It requires the ability to craft a narrative that not only resonates but also elevates, making the consumer believe they are buying more than just a product—they're investing in value, identity and trust. This is how brands justify higher price points, transcending the mere utility of their origins. The road to this transformation, however, is fraught with challenges.

Take consistency, for example: Commodities are often sourced from diverse suppliers, making it a Herculean task to maintain uniform quality across the board. Without meticulous supply chain management and rigorous quality control, even the strongest brand promise can falter. True brand alchemy demands more than marketing wizardry; it requires a seamless alignment of operations, strategy and storytelling.

Marketing gurus often preach this formula: Segment the market, craft a compelling value proposition, communicate it consistently and establish a resonant brand purpose. But this is easier said than done. Few examples capture this challenge as starkly as bottled water.

Once considered an absurd idea—why would anyone pay for what flows freely from taps?—Bisleri turned water into liquid gold, leading the market for decades and redefining consumer expectations.

Hemant Malik of ITC emphasizes that insights for branding extend far beyond consumer behaviour or market research. 'Trade research, competition analysis and supply chain mastery are equally critical before launching a product and building a brand. Otherwise, the product might meet a need but still fail spectacularly.' Gujarat Ambuja Cement exemplifies this philosophy. By addressing every facet of its business ecosystem—from sourcing to consumer messaging—it didn't just launch a cement brand; it revolutionized an industry, cementing its position as a market leader.

The power of storytelling is another linchpin in this metamorphosis. P.C. Musthafa of iD Fresh Food argues, 'A brand needs the right product, the right experience and stories that resonate deeply with customers.' Take salt, for instance—a commodity so ubiquitous, it once seemed impossible to brand. Yet, Tata Salt emerged as a household staple, its promise of purity making it the default choice for millions. But where there's a dominant player, there's also opportunity. Puro Salt carved its own niche by targeting consumers through heightened awareness, creating its own leadership narrative. Even gold, steeped in tradition and trust, often bought from family favoured retailers, was revolutionized by Tanishq. It didn't just sell gold; it sold assurance, innovation and a modern sensibility,

becoming the undisputed leader in its category.

The story repeats across kitchens nationwide, where staples like wheat flour still remain largely unbranded or dominated by hyperlocal players. 'This holds true for almost every product in the kitchen,' observes Vispy, who has conducted extensive research on consumer staples. Yet, when a powerhouse like ITC enters the scene, armed with its robust research and strategic prowess, the outcome is often a category-defining brand.

The lesson is clear: The magic of turning a commodity into a brand lies in seeing beyond the product itself. It's about finding the latent potential, crafting a unique promise and delivering on it consistently. This is not just branding—it's transformation. It's about creating a legacy where once there was only utility.

16

AASHIRVAAD: BRANDING THE COMMON WHEAT FLOUR

Let us look at a brand which has taken the market by storm. Faced with the enormous challenge of entering a category which was generic and largely undifferentiated, ITC went about systematically understanding customer needs and creating a product which suited those needs. All the elements of marketing were needed to make the brand a leader.

ITC's Aashirvaad is the amazing story of a brand reaching leadership levels in a commodity market. Despite its commanding position today, it continues to grow and add other categories like besan under the same umbrella brand.

We are warmly received by Nandini Basu, vice president, corporate communications, as we enter the imposing and grand building of the ITC headquarters in Virginia House, Kolkata. We then meet Hemant Malik, a genial man who comes to the point straightaway without wasting any time. A bespectacled gentleman with a thick moustache, he has recently been promoted to divisional chief executive, foods, and we congratulate him. He has been with ITC for decades and is one of the founding team members of ITC Foods. He smiles warmly and begins, 'Food is a category where the share of branded products varies based on the kind of food one is talking of.' He continues:

> For example, in the chocolates category, branded products make up nearly 95 per cent of the market, while for spices it is 55 per cent. But atta, wheat flour, even today, twenty years after we launched branded atta, brands contribute about 20 per cent of the total market. Loose and locally packaged wheat flour continue to rule the roost.

Hemant Malik remembers the date, 27 May 2002, when ITC launched Aashirvaad. He was the marketing manager then. He says, 'With a turnover of ₹9,000 crore in 2023, Aashirvaad has come a long way and will continue to grow.' Hemant explains the journey:

> When it comes to converting a commodity in the foods category into a brand, the marketer must look at all the elements of marketing which are based on various insights. Brands are not built by market research and positioning alone, but by trade research, competition research and research in trends and the understanding of technology. For example, the supply chain is a crucial element of success. Our field research showed that the consumer wants fresh atta, and while we have a shelf life of ninety days, the consumer doesn't want to pick up a pack which is more than thirty days old. Consumers are looking at the expiry date and how fresh the product is. This means that companies must manage their supply chain efficiently.

He explains how ITC ensures that production is close to the place of consumption.

When Aashirvaad was launched in 2002, there were many local brands and some other better-known nationally available brands like Shakti Bhog, Annapurna and Nature's Fresh. The price points were between ₹115 to ₹140 for a 10-kg pack of atta. 'In the foods category, ITC has a philosophy—if the product is not superior, there is no reason for the consumer to shift. So product quality was paramount,' says Hemant. 'Imagery and branding would not work unless the product is inherently superior. Consumers are willing to pay some premium for the "brand" when there is assurance of quality. This premium is not more than 5 per cent in foods.'

The first ask for ITC was to ensure the product was superior. The penetration of branded atta then was very poor—just 2 per cent or so. Explains Hemant, 'The consumer, that is the housewife, has to spend a lot of time and effort to buy the grain, take it to the chakki wallah, while also getting the endorsement from the in-laws, parents and husband. The housewife wants to ensure that her rotis come out soft.' The husband carries a lunch box to work, so the rotis must remain soft for several hours, market studies showed. ITC spent time understanding how to ensure that the rotis remained soft while having a hint of sweetness to it. ITC looked at two properties—water absorption property (WAP) and damaged starch (DS) property. ITC studied sharbati and other types of wheat from different parts of the country and found the right combination for a particular market. Research showed that people in southern India were not buying atta regularly. They would at most buy 1 kilogram of atta. Understanding what a roti stood for was crucial. ITC created a different blend for each of the regions. 'Today, we have different blends for Rajasthan, Bihar and many other states,' Hemant explains.

ITC first spent time understanding the product per se. Sourcing was supported by ITC Agri as they had a huge reach among farmers. 'But every year, we measure WAP and DS and other technical parameters, and the blender then ensures that the blend is consistent.

ITC has decades of experience in blending with tobacco. A smoker wants to get the same feel when he smokes his cigarette. The tobacco leaf used each year is not the same but with the right blend, we ensure that the consumer gets the same feel and taste. We are masters in blending.'

Marketing a simple product like atta is easy if it is a local shop, but when a brand has to go nationwide, with the assurance of quality coming from a company like ITC, a lot of elements of consistency need to be factored in.

The second challenge was to ensure the pricing was competitive. This is where supply chain, logistics, blend and other such factors were considered as ITC had realized that the consumer would not pay more than 5 per cent extra for Aashirvaad or any premium brand. But before she tried the brand, sampling would play a crucial role for a food product like atta to nudge the customer to try it. We had seen how Bahri Malhotra of Weikfield used sampling extensively to create a demand for his custard.

Hemant Malik elaborates:

> We served millions of samples for the consumer to try. Unless she tries the atta, we knew she would not convert to Aashirvaad. We wanted her to try it and experience it. After mass sampling, we did a conversion activity, where we would stand at marketplaces and urge the customer to buy the brand. For the food category, this was crucial.
>
> Shakti Bhog was a big brand in northern India. We started an 'atta challenge' where we would invite ladies and ask them to knead the flour with a blindfold on. After the kneading, we would ask her which one she liked. She would intuitively say Shakti Bhog, but then it would be revealed that it was actually Aashirvaad's consistency that she liked best. It was a nudge for her to reconsider her choice. In the blind test, she had clearly preferred Aashirvaad. ITC wanted to be a friend to the housewife in the kitchen. The reluctance towards buying a

> product like atta, which is fundamentally going to change the taste and hence her existence in the kitchen, is strong. It needs a push. It was important to ensure that Aashirvaad was seen as her support in the kitchen, an ally who would make her look good as a homemaker.

It is a strategy which works well when it comes to food. To become the homemaker's friend is a real test of a brand's success. We will see the same idea repeated in the story of iD Fresh Food.

ITC Foods continued to take feedback from the consumer to understand things like colour and texture. The process of innovation hadn't stopped.

Pricing was a crucial aspect in the product's success. The maximum retail price for branded atta was around ₹135 or so. The shopkeeper would offer something worth ₹30 free if a customer spent that amount. ITC decided to do away with these freebies and asked the trader to sell at ₹105, rather than go through the rigmarole of the freebie. 'We are an honest brand with honest pricing,' says Hemant, continuing:

> We didn't want to be seen as giving away freebies and then discounting the product. The retailer was given the atta at ₹95 and he would sell it at ₹105. This was seen as a refreshing change in the market. Visibility was crucial for sales. ITC came up with standees with wheels where the atta packs could be rolled up front. The atta bags were otherwise dumped at the back of the shop. The standee helped ensure that Aashirvaad literally stood out.

While the atta business looks easy enough to enter, it is difficult to sustain in the long run. One example was that of Hindustan Unilever, which sold its atta brand, Annapurna, in 2022, to a Singapore-based company. Hindustan Unilever was doing well in beauty and skincare, where the margins are high. With the food business, the margins are low, and it is not easy for a marketer to continue to succeed here. Hemant clarifies that ITC is not looking at market share in isolation but is all about growing the market. 'There is a huge potential for growth as the market is wide open,' he says.

Communication was another element which was crucial to success. 'In south India, Pilsbury was the largest brand, and one change in communication got ITC to nearly 90 per cent–plus market share in the south,' he says proudly.

When it comes to food, the marketer has to be aware of trends, fads and internet videos which suddenly become fashionable and promote a particular food or trash something else. While many of them may not be true or verifiable, the consumer gets swayed by these videos. Being aware of these trends and taking proactive action is what sets a brand leader apart. Hemant explains:

> There was a trend about rice not being healthy. Doctors were talking of adding more wheat to the diet. We didn't want to scare the customer. We used Bharatnatyam to depict active energy. The protagonist was a young Bharatnatyam dancer at her arangetram, her first public solo performance. The visuals of her billowing half-saree alongside fluffy rotis created an instant connection. ITC worked diligently on this concept, sponsoring Bharatnatyam arangetrams across southern India. We associated ourselves with the concept of 'active energy', and it has worked.[1]

He continues:

> Aashirvaad is about 'joyful nurturing'. We call it 'khushiyan chun chunke', where we select the grains from our 'e-choupal' network. ITC is the housewife's ally in the kitchen, we help her

---

1. We were unable to find the ad mentioned by Hemant on YouTube or any other social media.

get the best grain and the best atta so that she can feel proud when she makes rotis.

Today, Aashirvaad is growing fastest in the multigrain category. It is high in fibre which impacts digestion. We have made digestion mainstream. No one wants to talk about it—marketers have always shied away from talking about constipation. In our survey, we found that it was a real problem and needed to be addressed directly. And our communication showed just that. In the ad, parents ask the child coming out of the toilet, 'Hua kya?' The child shakes his head. After eating high-fibre rotis, the next day, the parents are pleased when the child comes out of the bathroom after having done his job!

Focus on high fibre, and we own the space of happy tummy.

In the south, ITC is trying to grow by expanding the market. The brand's penetration is high but the frequency of someone buying it is low as the consumer has atta only twice a week. Explains Hemant:

If we can increase that number to three times a week, our business would grow by 50 per cent. Rotis go only with kurma; it doesn't go well with sambar. So we created an ad called 'Tarun's tiffin', where we showed his tiffin as being the most coveted in the office. It shows the versatility of the product. In Bengaluru, ITC has started Namma Chakki, which helps the customer make her own atta.

ITC continues to research how a customer kneads her atta. How the brand and product talk to the consumer. It is all customized. And the ability to customize is the secret to success. But it is not easy to copy. 'We have thirty-five factories,' says Hemant. 'It is a high freight-intensive product. Our sourcing is our strength. And we continue to listen to the customer and keep improving.'

Hemant continues, 'Today [as of 2023], Aashirvaad is a ₹9,000 crore brand and has more than 45 per cent market share in the branded market at an all-India level, with more than 90 per cent share in the south.'

He calls ITC Foods a twenty-year-old start-up. It behaves like one, innovating constantly and listening to the customer's needs. Hemant concludes, 'With just 20 per cent of the market covered by branded attas, there is a tremendous scope for Aashirvaad and others to continue to grow.'

The story of Aashirvaad offers some fascinating insights on marketing strategy. It is a brand which has created a name for its consistent quality and purity, which has helped build trust among consumers. The brand ensures that its flour is made from the finest wheat, making it a reliable choice for households. Aashirvaad uses a unique 'fortification' process, where essential nutrients like iron, vitamin B12 and folic acid are added, contributing to the overall health of consumers and setting it apart from competitors. The brand's atta is known for producing soft, fluffy rotis, which has made it a popular choice for consumers seeking high-quality, smooth-textured flour. Keeping in mind customer preferences, Aashirvaad atta offers a wide range of products catering to different needs, such as whole wheat, multigrain, with millets and also a gluten-free variant. In food, as we saw in the story, it is important to maintain consistent quality and, over the years, Aashirvaad has established itself as a brand that consistently delivers, helping it build a loyal customer base. Consumers trust the brand for its commitment to quality and safety standards.

Aashirvaad's marketing campaigns often focus on the importance of family and home-cooked meals, resonating with the Indian values of togetherness and nourishment. Aashirvaad has used prominent chefs like Ranveer Brar as brand ambassadors, which has enhanced its visibility and appeal, particularly among urban consumers. Other elements of marketing, like a wide retail reach and e-commerce presence, are necessary today for a brand's success, and ITC has been able to leverage its nationwide network for the same. As we saw earlier, adapting to regional preferences, offering atta from coarse to finely milled flour is part of the marketing strategy to gain customer acceptance across India.

The success of Aashirvaad atta can be attributed to its focus on quality, health and trust, backed by strong brand equity, innovative marketing, wide distribution and adaptability to regional preferences. Its ability to address consumers' latent health concerns with fortified products and consistent delivery of premium quality has made it a household name in India.

ITC Foods is surely on the right path, not only multiplying business volumes but introducing brands in other food segments too.

17

GUJARAT AMBUJA CEMENT: CEMENTING A LEADERSHIP POSITION

As we saw in the story of Aashirvaad, creating a brand out of a commodity requires a deep understanding of consumer needs, backed by strong market research, and followed with other principles of marketing, all working in tandem. Gujarat Ambuja Cement had the same journey. Vispy and his team worked extensively with a product like cement. 'It is not a product you get up in the morning and think of,' Vispy says. 'To build a brand out of such a commodity was a huge challenge, and we had the help of the promoter, Narotam Sekhsaria, to make it happen.'

Creating a brand leader in a category identified as commodity requires the company to work on all parts of the product, as we saw in the case of household items like atta. When it comes to a product like cement, where the end customer is not involved and the decision-makers are masons or builders and architects, building a brand needs serious engagement on all fronts.

In his autobiography, *The Ambuja Story*,[1] Narotam Sekhsaria describes in great detail the journey of the cement company and how he became a cement manufacturer, despite starting out as a cotton trader.

When Gujarat Ambuja Cement was established, the single biggest challenge was to create a brand leader out of a product category which was seen as a commodity with no differentiation. Except ACC, the Associated Cement Companies, none of the other cement brands enjoyed any recall value.

Gujarat Ambuja Cement is a story in which all the elements of marketing were used well, leading to the creation of a brand leader. Very rarely does one see such a consistent effort to address all elements, culminating in a leadership position.

Research showed that a consumer merely asked for 'cement', without referring to any brand. This was the challenge Gujarat Ambuja wanted to overcome. One of the first things was that cement sold in the market was '33 grade'. This was a technical challenge to overcome as it was about the product attribute.

Market research had clearly shown that the customer wanted a 'strong' cement as they wanted a house, or anything else they built, to last for a long time—literally a lifetime. Hence, strength was an important criterion to work upon.

Narotam Sekhsaria writes in his book that the technical term was 'compressive strength'. For its measurement, a block of cement concrete of a predetermined size is prepared by mixing cement, sand and crushed stone, gravel and water in prespecified proportions, and is then cured by moistening it for a fixed number of days—in most cases, twenty-eight days.

A little bit of technical information here: A cement bag with Ordinary Portland Cement, OPC, 43 grade, meant that it will attain

1. Narotam Sekhsaria, *The Ambuja Story: How a Group of Ordinary Men Created an Extraordinary Company* (Gurgaon: HarperCollins India, 2021).

a minimum compressive strength of 43 megapascal pressure unit (MPa) in twenty-eight days. Similarly, OPC 53 would achieve a strength of 53 MPa in the same period. While this might sound very technical to a lay reader, it was an important criterion for the mason or the builder.

The best cement available in the market then had a strength of 43 MPa, and Sekhsaria decided to come out with Ambuja OPC 53 grade, which would become the yardstick against which all cement was measured.

With research insights making it clear that strength was the most important criterion, the question was how does one communicate that Gujarat Ambuja Cement was the best in its category? To do so, the advertising team brought out a hand-drawn visual of a man, with notably exaggerated biceps and shoulders, holding a dam comfortably in his giant-sized muscular arms. The advertisement didn't show any cement bags. The entire focus was on 'compressive strength'.

It was the tagline which made Gujarat Ambuja stand out. The mix of Hindi and English in the line 'virat compressive strength' clearly communicated what it stood for. The message was clear: Gujarat Ambuja stood for compressive strength. Adds Vispy:

> Research showed that the customer rarely asks for a compressive strength of 53 or 43. The mason doesn't specifically quote such numbers but he is surely looking for cement with strength. With consistent advertising, it was clear to the customer that Gujarat Ambuja was better and stronger than others. And he started asking for it by brand name.

The marketing team debated whether to use a male model in the advertisement—a muscular man, a Mr Universe of sorts. They concluded that the idea of using a graphic, and not an actual person, made sense. The moment a real model is shown, the viewer is able to ascribe a particular strength to him based on his physical features. But in Gujarat Ambuja's case, the graphic showed a huge man holding a dam or a tall building comfortably in his arms. The imagery clearly showed that the strength of Gujarat Ambuja stood, literally, heads and shoulders above other cement brands. Exaggeration worked!

But this alone was not enough, the research team had also concluded. Launching a brand with a certain positioning needs to be supported by other elements of marketing. Only then would the brand clearly differentiate itself against other cements.

The next step was to work on the distribution. While most cement manufacturers were selling through multi-brand cement stockists, Gujarat Ambuja decided to go for exclusive stockists. It was a difficult decision as it was against the market norms of the day. But the company assured stockists that it would drive customers to them. For the brand to stand out, it needed exclusivity. The dealers were initially worried but when customers started asking for Gujarat Ambuja, they realized that their exclusive status was working. This helped to create differentiation for the brand.

Another aspect to consider was pricing. The pricing was meant to suggest that it was a premium product, and the higher price worked in Gujarat Ambuja's favour as the customer perceived the brand as superior. Once a product achieves the status of premium, the absolute price ceases to have any meaning. Thanks to its advertising constantly reinforcing how strong its cement was, Gujarat Ambuja Cement was able to drive up its price.

The company didn't stop there but looked at all the elements of the business to ensure market leadership. For the first time, the company decided to transport cement by ship rather than by trucks. At the first factory in Kodinar, Gujarat, the trucks took the cement to the nearby port, where it was loaded onto a ship. In fact, they went a step further and loaded clinker, which would then be crushed in Mumbai or elsewhere, and made into cement powder. Not only did it result in cost efficiency but also allowed distribution in bulk.

Product packaging was another area in which Gujarat Ambuja showed innovation. Cement bags are otherwise undifferentiated. If the brand had to stand out, they needed to change the packaging as well. Gujarat Ambuja introduced paper bags for cement, which till then was sold in plastic bags. The biggest advantage was that they could print on paper. Moreover, with paper bags, the issue of someone using a hook to carry them didn't occur at all. With plastic bags, this was a common problem and would lead to leakage. Paper bags gave the brand the advantage of being able to put its brand name on it in an aesthetic manner.

All the elements of the brand—product, packaging, distribution and pricing—were used to differentiate the brand from others.

The animated giant in the ad—much like the Michelin man, the Duracell bunny or Gattu of Asian Paints—is timeless because it is not a human figure. It is unquantifiable, yet it showcases all the brand attributes.

The company's strategy was nothing short of a masterstroke. They didn't just market their cement, they wove it into the very foundation of trust within the industry. Instead of chasing the end customer directly, they turned their attention to the mason, the true gatekeeper of construction decisions. Research revealed a powerful truth: While the customer paid for the cement, it was the mason's word that sealed the deal. His endorsement was more than a recommendation, it was a commandment.

By understanding this, the company orchestrated a campaign that was both tactical and transformative. Workshops were not just educational sessions, they were immersive experiences designed to instil unwavering faith in the brand. They engaged with masons relentlessly, ensuring that every bag of cement they laid down was backed by conviction. This wasn't just marketing, it was a movement. The power of word of mouth took over, and soon the brand wasn't just another name in the market—it was *the* name.

In the end, the impossible had been achieved. What was once just another commodity had been elevated to an industry-defining brand. Gujarat Ambuja had cracked the code—transforming cement from an indistinguishable necessity into a symbol of reliability and strength. Few companies have ever managed such a feat. Every single aspect of marketing was not just accounted for but executed with precision. The result? A brand that didn't just lead the market, it ruled it—standing unchallenged for decades.

The Gujarat Ambuja story is not just about cement. It is about transformation, about turning an ordinary commodity into an extraordinary brand. It is a testament to the sheer power of strategic marketing and razor-sharp business acumen. Gujarat Ambuja Cement didn't just enter the market, it redefined it. In an industry where cement was seen as just another raw material, the brand shattered the mould by emphasizing its superior strength, durability and consistency, standing tall above the competition.

From the outset, the company played a bold game, opting for exclusive dealerships that gave it an air of prestige and an undeniable edge. But it didn't stop there. Gujarat Ambuja revolutionized logistics, creating an ironclad supply chain with bulk shipping, dedicated rail routes and private ports. The result? A drastic reduction in transportation costs, lightning-fast delivery and an unparalleled market reach.

The brand didn't just sell cement, it built a legacy. Through unforgettable advertising campaigns, it etched its name into the minds of consumers, associating itself with unbreakable strength and reliability. More than that, it educated the very hands that shaped the industry—masons, contractors and engineers—ensuring they not only understood the benefits of its cement but swore by it. Workshops weren't just training sessions, they were relationship-building power moves, forging loyalty that would stand the test of time.

Gujarat Ambuja's meteoric rise was no accident. It was the result of visionary branding, an unwavering commitment to quality and an unrelenting drive for efficiency and innovation. What was once just another cement company rose to become an industry titan, setting benchmarks, inspiring competitors and cementing, quite literally, its place as a market leader for generations to come.

Incidentally, Holcim, a Swiss group, bought Gujarat Ambuja Cement in 2006. Later, it was bought by the Adani Group.

18

TANISHQ: A TRUST EARNED OVER TIME

A house is one of the biggest investments a person makes in his lifetime. And cement plays a big role in the construction of houses. We saw how Gujarat Ambuja created a brand from a commodity like cement. While most household savings are used for building a home, the other event where most Indian households spend maximum money from their savings—and in many cases, sadly, by borrowing—is their child's wedding. Think of a wedding and you would imagine the customer going to a trusted jeweller. And when it comes to trust, what better brand than Tata?

But it was not all smooth sailing when the Tatas launched Tanishq—a market leader in the gold jewellery business today.

Now, when you look at Tanishq, it is difficult to believe that the brand and business were a failure when they first launched. Trust builds over time, and that is why millions of Indians tended to flock to their local jeweller whom they had trusted for generations. Titan decided to challenge that, and failed! Little did the management at Titan realize that trust in the Tata brand alone would not work and that they would have to understand the customer's mindset before they could establish trust. That is what Tanishq did. Today, it is surely a brand which falls in the consideration category. It is not only a leader in most markets, but it also stands for quality, purity and transparency—all important parameters when dealing with precious metals and stones.

~

Tanishq is the unique story of a brand which, when launched, despite enormous potential and industry size, was a failure in the Titan world and planned to be shut down. Market research, diligent efforts and an understanding of what the customer wanted not only turned the brand around but made it a superhero in its category.

'For the first three years since its launch, Tanishq floundered and the board had almost decided to close down the business,' recalls Jacob Kurian, who had been given one year to prove whether the business was worth keeping. It was a chance comment by one of the board members of Titan, a TIDCO (Tamil Nadu Industrial Development Corporation, a JV partner of Titan) representative a gentleman from Chennai, who remarked that he sees enormous crowds at the traditional jewellers in Chennai, that led to Jacob concluding that the market was there. Titan just didn't know how to address it. And he had one year to change all that!

Tanishq, the brainchild of the very dapper Xerxes Desai, the erstwhile CEO of Titan Industries, had been established for very different reasons—like earning forex and to foray into international markets. Titan and Xerxes never had plans to dominate India when the brand was launched.

'The design team and the CEO were oriented towards "international", and the designs which Tanishq launched in India were considered "trinkety". A customer went to Tanishq for trinkets—bracelets, earrings, etc., but when it came to the "main" jewellery, meaning jewellery for weddings and such events, it was the local jeweller that the customer preferred,' explains Santosh Desai, who did extensive research for Tanishq. Santosh, himself an ad veteran and someone with deep knowledge of consumer insights, loves to tell stories from a buyer-behaviour perspective.

'Tanishq was selling 18-carat gold, presuming that since it was popular in Western countries, it would sell here too. But in India, it was seen as cheap. People wanted 22-carat gold. Moreover, the African-American models used in the earlier ads did not resonate with the Indian customers,' Santosh adds.

The research team decided to address the issues with a first-principles approach. While it was evidently clear, as the board member's remark suggested, that the market itself was large and that customers were flocking to traditional shops, there was a need to understand what 'culture' meant. Tanishq had to take a serious view to understand the customer.

'A brand is a junction of meanings,' Santosh explains. What he meant was that the entire Tanishq brand had to be reconsidered; they had to ask themselves what they stood for in the minds of the customer.

The research took place using consumer immersion in ten major cities, apart from lot of other secondary research which included understanding emerging trends, what 'gold' meant in India, talking to experts of culture like Devdutt Pattanaik and asking questions like, 'What is the place of jewellery in Indian culture?'

'The idea was to break down the elements of the brand, disaggregate them and then put them together to form a cohesive whole which appealed to the customer,' Santosh elaborates as he talks about Tanishq's journey, how it went upwards from its lowest point.

This is where Jacob Kurian and his team stepped in. Jacob had been given the unenviable task of brand turnaround. When he was given this role, he was working in Titan's watch division and, having won the ET Brand Equity award that particular year, he felt that he was given a task he was sure to fail at. Not to mention, he would have to face the mocking of his colleagues who believed Tanishq was a joke.

Handed a deadline that loomed just one year away, Jacob wondered what he should do. 'I parked my car outside Bhima Jewellers, a huge jeweller in Bengaluru, and then walked to our shop on Dickenson Road,' Jacob recalls. 'The crowds at Bhima, just like the crowds at the Chennai jewellers, as the board member had mentioned to me, reinforced to me again that the business was there. In contrast, we had not a single customer in our shop! Clearly, we didn't know what and how to sell, and we were not doing things right.'

Jacob and his team got down to understanding the customer and their needs. The initial research, which showed that there was a huge market, was scrapped, as that was a pretty obvious point. Another piece of research showed that, contrary to the internal belief of Titan executives, brand Tanishq enjoyed 75 per cent recall and that more advertising was not needed. 'The biggest perception was that Tanishq was six to seven times more expensive than other brands,' says Jacob with a chuckle. 'Quite obviously, this was far from the truth and highly exaggerated, but then perception is reality, and we had to accept it and find a way to change that.'

Tanishq's approach of using Indian jewellery (instead of European and Western designs) and introducing the Karatmeter (a device which showed the purity of the gold with a non-destructive testing method), coupled with the brand's trust factor had shown some encouraging results. But it was nowhere near what the board wanted. Clearly, a lot had to be done.

'*Jewellery is like a watch for the customer*—this is what Titan executives had earlier assumed,' says Jacob. 'We thought that the emotional involvement of a customer buying jewellery was akin to buying a watch. We were completely wrong.'

Jacob's research showed that, for women, buying jewellery was a highly emotional decision and was about 'I, me, mine'. Research brought out the issue that the decision to buy was often 'design-induced' but the act of buying jewellery was essentially a complex emotion. Jacob tells us:

> Jewellery was a strange kind of consumer durable purchase, which was worn for style, but the buying rationale had many

> layers to it. These included being an investment, a family heirloom, a source of income during an emergency, and such. In a Tanishq advertisement, a lady throws her jewellery on the floor because she didn't like it and because it was earlier close to her heart but was now worthless. Women, when asked in consumer-insight studies about the advertisement, said it was insulting and hurt their emotions. We realized the kind of involvement women had with jewellery. We couldn't afford to insult them. We didn't know what to do. There were all these elements of the brand to be considered for it to become a success. There were so many times I wondered why I had taken the job when I could have been cruising along in my job in watch sales.

A lot of mystery shopping was done to understand how other jewellers were selling and what the customer was looking for. Jacob recalls going to a big local jeweller asking for a chain. The salesperson quickly realized that he was merely window shopping and continued to focus on the family standing next to Jacob, who had come to buy wedding jewellery. Jacob realized that Tanishq faced a problem of arrogance, wherein they believed in telling the truth and leaving it to the customer to presume that they were the best. Tanishq had an element of trust which was evident, but it was not translating to sales. They were not speaking the 'sales language'.

Jacob talks about Karatmeter: 'Undercartage is an industry problem. It is something that has been around for decades, and it doesn't seem to be going away soon either.'

The Karatmeter story begins when Vasant Nangia, during a routine visit to a factory, spotted an X-ray fluorescence machine that used spectroscopy to measure 'cartage'. The company came out with print ads which said, 'Beware, there is a thief in the family.' While it was a move in transparency, allowing the customer to see for themselves the quality of the gold bought, it was not helping sales. The Karatmeter had been around for a couple of years by then, but despite its apparent non-destructive testing, it was not leading to conversions. Jacob recalls a woman storming out of his store saying the Karatmeter was of no help as it only made her feel horrible because, thanks to the instrument, she had now realized she had been cheated by her family jeweller many years ago. She wanted a *solution*. She did not only want to be told that her jewellery was not as pure as she had thought it to be. When Jacob asked the lady how he could help, she shouted, 'You don't have any solutions! You just want to make people feel bad.' She stormed out after that. Just viewing the results had upset her. Jacob started thinking of ways to address her problem.

Once again, an interaction in the market had shown why most women didn't come forward to test their jewellery. Jacob also realized how similar their situation was to what was seen in a survey conducted by a medical company: most women don't go for mammograms as there was no cure for the cancer, and they would also be facing a potential loss in their femininity if their breasts were to be removed. He continues:

> Jewellery was considered a family-run business, where the promoter knows the customer and her family for generations. Jewellery was a generational tradition wherein the grandmother handed over her jewels to the granddaughter or the daughter-in-law. When asked how they trusted the jeweller who was apparently cheating them, the answer was always, 'They don't cheat *us*; they may be cheating someone else!' There was no logic to it, but the customer still trusted the family jeweller. There had to be a way to make the Karatmeter work. After all, it was a device which proved the authenticity of the gold.

This issue was addressed after considering market feedback. A scheme called 'Impure to Pure' was launched in which the customer could bring her jewellery to a Tanishq store, melt it down, sell it to the brand

and, in lieu of the money offered, buy new jewellery which was made of pure gold. The scheme took off in a big way. 'I recall being called urgently to our store in Bengaluru. I thought it was another customer problem but, to my surprise, I found crowds at the store. The scheme had worked and soon word of mouth helped bring in business. We had arrived at one part of the solution,' Jacob says with pride.

> The staff was unable to handle the billing and the queues. There were that many people crowding the store! The scheme had succeeded. The lady who had stormed out of my store had given me that insight. Our Karatmeter, our trust, our transparency had worked wonders, and more and more customers came and experienced how we were different and better than other local jewellers.
>
> We had learnt about assortment planning, adjacencies and many other things to create the whole experience leading to sales. We also assumed that the purity issue would not be a long-term differentiator for us as the government was also talking of hallmark. It took many more years for it to become a hygiene factor as the jewellers—many of them, in fact—continued to cheat their customers. It was, and is, too tempting, as there are too many gullible customers.

Y.L. Saroja, former head of design and marketing at Tanishq, says, 'While there have been many other studies by industry bodies talking about the lower gold purity levels in the market, the exchange scheme run by Tanishq reinforced the findings.'[1]

Coming back to the story. 'All the elements of the brand needed to come together to make Tanishq a blockbuster, and there were

1. 'Tanishq reopens 'Impure to Pure Exchange Offer' till 30 June', Domain B, 17 June 2003, https://www.domain-b.com/ companies/companies_t/tanishq/20030617_reopens.htm, accessed on 3 April 2025.

many still missing or not aligned to the Titan vision,' explains Jacob. He reiterates what he learnt from marketing gurus:

> The price perception of Tanishq was addressed when we began hiring people from other jewellers. We were arrogant in telling the customer about the making charges. A salesperson told me that we should say, "Starting from ₹40", which was true for the factory-made bangle. He said we shouldn't say our making charge is a flat so-and-so per gram. We were, in reality, cheaper than the local jeweller but we were not using the right language.
>
> It was a factory worker who suggested a gold-saving scheme, and we launched that next. It worked well as we got a lot of working capital, cheaper than our other borrowing channels. The scheme is now worth hundreds of crores.

He continues:

> What we liked was that we emulated the industry practice, but we differentiated the brand by doing simple but remarkable things like keeping our shops open all days of the week. This was contrary to the other jewellers who were closed on Sundays as the promoter needed a day off. For us, it was not a problem. Soon, we attracted a lot of customers. We had changed an industry habit by being the first ones to be open all seven days of the week. We also changed the perception that a family jeweller does well if he knows the customer personally, by name, and knows their entire family, and that he can take pricing decisions on the fly. Our trust, purity and designs were working. The price perception that we were six to seven times more expensive was gone but it took a long time.
>
> An interesting insight we got from a study was that a woman bought most of her jewellery from 1.75 stores—that is

> around two stores at the most, of which one store (of the two) was responsible for 75 per cent of the sales. Thus, we needed to be just one of the two stores.

Tanishq realized that it didn't have to compete with twenty stores. If they could be part of the two stores in the customer's mind, they would get enough customers. Jacob explains:

> Sundays worked for us when we observed through mystery shopping that when a woman comes in with her husband, the sale is more likely to happen. Husbands are free on Sundays and are very reluctant to agree to one more round of window shopping for their fastidious wives! He is happy that his wife can complete all her shopping in Tanishq. All he does is fish out his credit card or a wad of notes—and the job is done. He is relieved! He likes the logical side of Tanishq, as it is transparent and clean, with no hanky-panky. The wife is happy that she gets pure gold with great designs. Sundays were an advantage for Tanishq and a disadvantage for the traditional jeweller, who needed to be personally present for the sale and couldn't delegate the work. It was a tactical decision, and it worked.

Sometimes, just walking around shows you what research can fail to. Jacob was in a store in Hyderabad once when he found an irate customer with a custom order, paid in advance; he was now being told the order would not be ready in time for his son's wedding. Quite naturally, he was mad and was willing to take the shop down in his fury. On enquiry, Jacob was surprised to find that the sales staff were reluctant to take custom orders, despite the advantages of a confirmed sale, as they didn't trust the factory producing the goods in time. Jacob tried understanding the problem at the factory level. There, he was even more shocked to learn that an order from Ratan Tata's office itself had been delayed and that there had been phone calls from Bombay House, the historic headquarters of the Tata Group, enquiring about it! Something needed to be done. The factory configuration needed to be redesigned.

'We were the first ones in the world to introduce Lean techniques in the manufacturing of jewellery. This brought about radical changes, and custom orders were now being produced as per the requirement,' Jacob explains. A simple observation in the market, followed by a technical analysis which provided a solution had led to a radical improvement in the business.

C.K. Venkataraman, or Venkat, the bespectacled CEO of Titan Ltd, was the marketing head around 2005 or so. We meet him in his Bengaluru head office. He tells us how Tanishq was able to address the different segments of the market:

> We realized through our extensive research, and also through feedback from our franchisees and store staff, that there were not only different state groups which had different tastes in jewellery but that there were also different communities within a particular language group itself. We then came out with designs to offer a traditional trousseau which appealed to that particular group. This resonated well with our customers as they felt we were listening to them and offering what they wanted.

Another insight gained was about the fact that Indians loved to save. According to Venkat (or CKV, as he is also often referred to):

> We were not using the scheme, which we called 'Golden Harvest', to get new customers but were targeting existing customers to entice them to save now and buy later. It worked wonders. A huge number of customers came back to us after making their initial purchase and enrolling for the scheme. Today, it is a building block for us as nearly 35 per cent of our sales comes from this scheme.

Venkat talks of how all the staff at the stores were trained after they gleaned insights into what the customer was expecting:

> Earlier, our staff would be aloof and would let the customer stroll in and walk around, and they would reach out only when asked for. We realized through our research that the customer was looking for an 'expert', someone who could guide her and tell her what she really wanted to buy. We trained our staff extensively in our long 'customer-centricity' training programmes. The staff was seen as friendly, accessible, approachable and, more importantly, as experts who could guide, without pushing the customers too hard. Of course, the training included helping them identify the kind of customer who walked in. There are many who don't want to be approached right away as they need their personal space. We trained our staff to understand these traits and act accordingly.

When CKV, then the marketing head, asked Santosh Desai to look into customer perception and carry out extensive research, the end result was a communication series called 'revitalizing tradition'.

'The brand may have emerged a hero in many markets, but Tanishq was struggling in Kerala, Tamil Nadu and a few other markets,' says Ajoy Chawla, CEO of the jewellery division. (He was later made the managing director of Titan on 1 January 2026.) Market research showed that Tanishq needed to be relevant to the customer in that region.

> Taking on Nayanthara as a brand ambassador was only a part of the campaign. We wanted to connect with the Tamil Nadu customer and we started Project Sigaram (meaning 'peak'), which was about achieving leadership. Region-specific jewellery and designs were key to success, without taking away the Tanishq experience, which had to be consistent across India.

Using consumer insights, Tanishq came up with a strategy to address the customer by decoding her 'need states'. CKV adds, 'We identified need states as that of everyday and occasion-based, like engagements, apart from things like faith, gents and kids. They all needed to be addressed differently.' Tanishq launched a campaign called 'Pudhumai Penn', which was about progressive women who were not just the upholders of tradition but change agents. 'Embracing tradition on one side and newness on the other,' the ad said.

Their research showed that young people choose engagement rings on their own, while the entire family was involved when it came to the purchase of wedding jewellery. The idea was to involve the customer from the time of their engagement to the wedding to their first anniversary. The focus on solitaires for special occasions and engagements reaped dividends.

Another insight the Tanishq team got was after they used Deepika Padukone and other celebrities as their brand ambassadors. Ajoy Chawla tells us:

> Our customers were telling us that they didn't need celebrity endorsement for Tanishq. They were telling us that they themselves were the largest brand ambassadors and their word-of-mouth advertising mattered. We did away with celebrities, except using people like Nayanthara for states like Tamil Nadu. We had a campaign called 'Every Woman Is a Diamond' in which we used real women as models. This helped us further our cause of Tanishq being a more authentic brand. In the jewellery market, authenticity and trust are huge gaps. The competition is opaque, but Tanishq has been consistent in its approach in highlighting this issue. We are about design differentiation, customer experience, trust and wholesomeness.
>
> We used our research feedback to talk about artisans and the invisible people who work behind the scenes to create the purity of Tanishq. Our 'Dua Ka Sona' campaign, which was about getting the blessings of the artisans working on the gold, resonated with the customer.

Tanishq has a long way to go. While it has an overall 7–8 per cent market share in India, there are states where we are very small, like Kerala, for example.

Bombay House refused to allow Tanishq to use the Tata name in the early 2000s.

This was an irony because, as of March 2024, sales of the jewellery division for Titan stood at more than a whopping ₹40,000 crore as per the company's balance sheet![2] Titan is the second-most valuable company in the Tata Group, after TCS.[3]

Unsung heroes like Jacob make a difference using observation, insights and their sheer dedication and determination to succeed.[4]

Tanishq is not just a brand, it is a saga of patience, keen market insight and an unyielding commitment to understanding consumer desires. It is a riveting tale of innovation, trust-building and bold strategies in an industry steeped in tradition and fragmentation. Tanishq didn't merely enter the jewellery market, it transformed it. By breaking away from the murky, opaque pricing practices of traditional jewellers, it introduced transparent pricing and weight-based billing, forcing the industry to play by new, fairer rules. In a market where gold purity was often shrouded in doubt, Tanishq took a revolutionary step with the Karatmeter. This pioneering device allowed customers to verify the authenticity of their jewellery, making Tanishq a beacon of trust in a landscape clouded with scepticism.

---

2. *Annual Reports,* Titan, https://www.titancompany.in/investors/annual-reports, accessed on 3 April 2025.
3. Watch sales, in contrast, are a mere 10 per cent, at around ₹3,900 crore! The watch company is now a jewellery company!
4. The authors consider it unfortunate that Jacob Kurian was not made CEO of Titan.

But the brand's innovation didn't stop at transparency. Tanishq understood the pulse of its customers and crafted collections that seamlessly blended heritage with contemporary elegance. Whether through Rivaah, its wedding-jewellery line steeped in tradition, or Mia, a bold statement for modern working women, the brand spoke to every woman's aspirations. Aligning itself with the Tata Group's reputation for integrity and ethics, Tanishq slowly but surely gained the credibility needed to challenge an industry often tainted by unethical practices.

Tanishq didn't just sell jewellery—it sold stories, emotions and cultural pride. Its advertising campaigns struck a deep chord with Indian consumers, portraying jewellery as more than an ornament—rather, a marker of love, celebration and heritage. Iconic campaigns, such as the one normalizing second marriages, broke stereotypes and resonated with progressive Indian women. The brand catered to brides, working professionals and families alike, ensuring an expansive reach. In its stores, Tanishq redefined luxury retail, offering not just exquisite jewellery but an experience—one of warmth, expert guidance and unparalleled customer service. Even when faced with controversy, such as the backlash over its ads featuring interfaith relationships, Tanishq stood resilient, skilfully navigating challenges without compromising its core values.

The success of Tanishq lies in its masterful fusion of tradition and modernity. It redefined jewellery retail with a rare combination of innovation, transparency and emotional resonance. By consistently evolving with the times while honouring cultural roots, Tanishq has not only earned trust, it has also become an aspirational icon for millions of Indians.

As the senior management of Titan believes, Tanishq's journey, in fact, has just begun. Tanishq is a leader—yet it has a long way to go, with many more milestones to reach.

19

iD FRESH: A REVOLUTION IN THE KITCHEN

We have explored so many brands that were adopted by customers for filling a gap they didn't know they had. But there are some things, especially when it comes to certain food products, that a woman would just not want to buy, but rather make herself.

The research on many food products done by Vispy and team showed consistently that the housewife always preferred homemade items. But things are changing with more women now working rather than just being a homemaker. Vispy elaborates, 'Branded spices, as per our research, constitute 35 per cent of the overall spice market in the country. The total spice market, including packaged and loose spices, as per many estimates, currently stands at ₹90,000 crore. Nevertheless, branded masalas are a fast-growing category as they bring a lot of convenience. There is enormous scope for brands in this category.'

But let's turn our focus to idlis and dosas—a daily staple in not just south Indian homes but homes across India these days. The housewife makes the idli or dosa batter at home and is hesitant to buy it from the local kirana shop. Even when she buys the batter, she is unsure of its consistency and the quality and purity of the ingredients used. Hence, she cannot always be sure that the idlis or dosas will turn out right. This is the insight that P.C. Musthafa hit upon, which made iD Fresh Food the leader in its category. The positioning of the brand was not something that Musthafa developed overnight; he gleaned it only after having studied consumer behaviour while he continued to sell his idli–dosa batter.

We meet him in his office in Bengaluru for a discussion over some coffee (another iD Fresh product) and to listen to him talk about how he made the brand a leader.

~

Identify a lucrative, unorganized category, set up scalable operations and enter with a convenient branded product: FMCG companies have been following this playbook for decades. Seen this way, iD Fresh Food's business model does not seem particularly unique. How, then, is the brand such a runaway success?

It was during a chance visit to a cousin's store for P.C. Musthafa, the founder of iD Fresh Food, that an idea took shape in his mind. His cousin ran a kirana shop and would stock idli batter from a local vendor. The batter would be sold in a plastic pouch, with a rubber band tied around its neck to seal it. The quality could never be guaranteed, and was found to vary with the weather and the kind of rice used to make the batter. *Why not provide consistent quality to the customer,* Musthafa mused.

Armed with this idea, Musthafa started the business with a small 50-square-foot kitchen in 2005 in Bengaluru. But it was only some months later that he and his team understood the importance of food technology in packaged foods.

He recounts, 'On a hot day in April 2006, I got a call from a store near Indiranagar in Bengaluru. I was told that there's been a an explosion in the store, and to come immediately.' Every entrepreneur dreams about the market for their products exploding. But what if the product itself explodes?

Musthafa and his team initially thought that the store manager was joking.

> We laughed, at first. We said, 'If you had a bomb blast in your store, please call the nearest police station; we don't handle bombs.' But it quickly became clear that the manager was furious. My team rushed to the store. The manager was very angry. He said, 'Go clean my fridge; take all the leftover batter and go home.' The idli batter packet had exploded!

Musthafa's team—consisting of his cousin and a salesperson—however, was not keen to give up so easily. The salesperson took a pack of batter to the store manager to try to convince him about the quality of their products. 'Before my salesman could finish—boom! This pack of batter exploded as well—leaving white batter on the manager's face.' Musthafa squirms, remembering the day.

It did not take him and his team long to figure out the reason for the 'explosion'—and the solution for it. 'Batter ferments during the summer. It expands, forms gas and, after a point, explodes. We had no idea about food technology before we started this business. In fact, I learnt about this term, "fermentation", only after this incident,' Musthafa confesses to us.

He realized that he had to improve his process if he were to avoid such disasters. Also, there was a need to experiment in a much larger market where he would be able to make a mark. This is what brought him to Chennai. The team had refined their process in the meanwhile and felt comfortable that they were ready with a better product.

A desire to succeed against all odds and a deep-rooted value system are not mutually exclusive, as far as Musthafa was concerned. His goal of making a mark in the Chennai market—considered the Mecca of idlis—in particular, posed the toughest challenge that the team had faced yet. 'We had created world's best batter and then, naturally, we thought why don't we go to Chennai?' he says. iD Fresh started operations in the city and quickly realized that it was a very tough market to break into. 'We had even invested in a factory there,' he adds.

To Musthafa's dismay, he found that unbranded batter was available for ₹10 a kg, compared to the one sold by iD Fresh at ₹45 a kg. Curious, Musthafa and his team tried to find out how their rivals were able to sell batter so cheap. He found out that the unbranded players were buying rice from ration shops that was available at ₹1 per kg and were making the idlis fluffier by adding large amounts of soda. There were three options available for Musthafa and his team: 'One was to follow this unethical, unhealthy practice, but we didn't want to take that shortcut. The second option was to borrow money on interest. With a larger scale we could have possibly brought down our prices a little, but we couldn't take that route because it was against my value system. Finally, the third option was to shut down the factory,' he says.

While Chennai was undoubtedly a lucrative market for idli batter, there was no way iD Fresh could have competed in a fair manner with the batter that was being sold locally. This left Musthafa to grapple with the toughest option. 'We decided to shut down the factory, sold all the assets and machineries and decided to come back. We had to accept such tough decisions in our life but the courage to take such decisions helped us create the strong brand that we are today.' He continues, adding with aa chuckle, 'It was better to not get battered over batter!'

Musthafa and his team focused on Bengaluru and continued to build their brand there. The business was doing well and they were making progress. But Musthafa was looking for an idea which would make his brand stand apart from the competition. The aha moment was yet to come.

It was about a decade later that the team decided to brainstorm ideas when the company had started doing well. The central idea following their discussion revealed the core concept of 'liberation'. The brand's values lay in being Indian, being rooted in tradition, open to ideas, modern and natural. The brand believed it was traditional, and smart, confident, contemporary and practical, like the women consumers they were targeting. The iD offered authentic taste, freshness and convenience, while appealing to the emotional aspect of the lady of the house providing for her family and being unwilling to compromise on quality. iD reiterated the same with their short shelf life, and their chemical-free and 100 per cent natural claim, along with quality ingredients in superior packaging. The '100 per cent natural' claim was a differentiator.

Taking the stance of not adding chemicals makes delivery challenging—especially for an unstable fermented product such as batter. It also comes at an extra cost, which is tricky for a brand like iD that wants to remain affordable. Musthafa explains:

> Because innovation, by definition, implies that something is being done for the first time, brands that innovate not only get talked about but are also perceived as leaders. This gives you a psychological edge in the consumer's mind. Let me give you one example of our innovation in transportation. Transporting batter over long distances affects the taste and quality of the batter. Inspired by the ready-mix concrete model, iD transports packed batter pre-fermentation, allowing it to ferment in a controlled environment along the way.

Research showed that the idli- and dosa-making process for housewives differed widely, and the main issue was getting consistently good quality ingredients. The right atmosphere, temperature for fermentation and grinding technology ensured that the batter was not consistent on a day-to-day basis, spoiling the end product. iD, with its unique sourcing and technology, ensured that all these problems were resolved without using any preservatives and using 100 per cent natural ingredients.

The new-generation housewife wanted her batter to be a consistent quality but she didn't want the drudgery of grinding the batter every few days at home.

Says Musthafa:

> Traditional wet-stone grinders make the best batter. However, they are slow and labour-intensive. Most high-performance industrial food-processing machines are made in Germany, but there was no ready equivalent for the Indian stone grinder. iD identified a mustard paste machine that worked a similar way and customized it to grind 5,000 kilos of batter per hour.'

The positioning and emotional appeal of iD was consistent. According to Musthafa:

> We wanted to reiterate that the housewife, the homemaker, was the provider of food, while iD was only a professional assistant for her chores. We were not taking away any credit due to her. If the idlis came out well, she would be congratulated, and if they didn't, she could conveniently blame it on the iD batter. The homemaker believes in the goodness of tradition but doesn't always have the time for it. This was a gap we were addressing. The target was the busy and smart woman, over twenty-five years in age, the gatekeeper, who hates making compromises when it comes to food.

Research showed that the customer used the product differently in different markets. A Kannadiga homemaker would use the batter for idlis on day one, make dosas or uthappams from it in another few days and then, when the batter was four to five days old, she would make paniyarams. On the other hand, in Tamil Nadu, the consumer would buy the batter which was nearing expiry to make idlis out of it.

Why didn't iD go for a separate batter for idlis and dosas, we ask Musthafa, who explains:

We realized that we wanted to give the homemaker a choice in terms of how she wants to use the batter. Most would use it for either idli or dosa, based on the household demand. And while we may lose out on a small proportion of customers who insist on having different batters, we find that more than 90 per cent of our customers are happy with a single batter. It was different for the vada, of course. It was a different recipe altogether. The vada batter has been a success since its launch. When the vada comes out, perfectly round, out of the vada-batter dispenser, that is the aha moment for the customer. We didn't sell vadas but let the housewife make vadas out of our batter. They turn out crisp on the outside, and soft and fluffy inside. They taste yummy! The product is clearly the hero. It is even a case study at Harvard Business School now.

We have been growing by 70 per cent in the last eighteen months, and while we are targeting an 80 per cent market share in Bengaluru, we are now present in forty-seven cities. There is a long way to go before we can say we have captured the market, but we are clearly the leader.

'The consumer believes in our promise of purity. We also stand for certain values—and we won't compromise on that,' Musthafa says, recalling a situation way back in 2011. They had launched a diamond-cut wafer product, shaped like a mini samosa. The chilli-flavoured product received an encouraging reception in the market and the demand started growing briskly. Musthafa elaborates:

One day, we got a call from one of the big hotels in Bengaluru and they said they wanted to buy thousands of kilos of diamond cuts. We first thought we had hit a jackpot, but I was curious to know why he was placing such a big order. Upon enquiring, the chef said that they wanted to create a bar snack using the wafers and serve it with alcohol. That is where

> the bulb lit up for me. We refused the deal, despite it being tempting financially, because of the values we stand for.

Musthafa says that he did feel like crying that day as it was hurting the company's bottom line, but he stuck to his core values as he knew that, in the long term, his brand could not be associated with alcohol.

Refusing money that is already on the table needs conviction in terms of one's values and what the brand stands for.

Another core value for the brand is transparency. Musthafa got the chance to demonstrate how important this value is for him in 2021, when viral social media posts claimed iD Fresh allegedly had animal extracts in its products.

'Every crisis is an opportunity for a village boy like me,' Musthafa explains, talking of his childhood in Kerala. He elaborates:

> We opened up our factory for a live tour and livestream. We had nothing to lose and everything to gain by showing to our customers how we made our products. We had nothing to hide. One of my professors at IIM had once told me about the difference between a rat and an elephant. If a rat wants to cross MG Road in Bengaluru, the professor explained, the rodent can take shortcuts and no one would notice. On the other hand, if an elephant wanted to cross the road, the world would definitely take notice. We were the elephant, and we decided to be transparent. It worked!

As an aside, Musthafa lists three attributes he has developed from growing up in a village, which have become a part of his DNA. 'Values, humility and jugaad … Earning money the right way and for the right cause is extremely crucial. A tree, laden with fruit, will always bend low. This is what your village and your family teach you,' he says.

Musthafa found a product that was being made at home, converted it into a brand with convenience without taking away any credit from the consumer, and made his brand a leader.

'If we can get the technology right, the next blockbuster for us is ready-made rotis, which just need to be heated,' he says. We are sure iD Fresh will find the solution soon.

They have already captured a niche with their bread, which has 100 per cent natural ingredients and no preservatives. But the idea of rotis, which are consumed by millions of customers, is an idea waiting for its time to come.

'Our customers trust us, and we wanted to reciprocate this trust,' Musthafa says. He tells us about iD Trust Shops, which he started during the COVID-19 pandemic.

He opens with a scenario: April 2020, Oberoi Park View apartments, Kandivali, Mumbai. The ritual starts around 7.30 a.m. Every morning, a white Maruti Omni enters Oberoi Park View. The driver, who is accompanied by a helper, parks the car, leaves the doors wide open and steps out of the society. Residents then form a queue while maintaining social distancing, pick up packed ready-to-make breakfast products, such as idli/dosa batter, parotta and paneer from the car—as many packs as they want. The ritual is unusual for many reasons: There is no salesperson collecting money, no security guard manning the van, no vending machine installed to deposit money. And there's nobody keeping a tab of how many packs each resident is picking up. The vehicle is one of forty-two at multiple locations in Mumbai that follow the same routine every morning. To an outsider, it would seem like a charitable act against the backdrop of the nationwide lockdown since March 2020. Seven months on, the vans kept coming and the goods vanished within an hour or so, even as nobody really keeps a watch.

P.C. Musthafa, though, knows somebody is.

'God is watching,' he says. He started these vans, known as Trust Shops, as a pilot programme across 500 resident welfare associations (RWAs) in Mumbai, in April 2020. If the idea was simple—an innovative way to beat the pandemic blues as retail stores were shuttered—the thought behind it was equally elementary: Trust the consumers.

'It has to be 100 per cent trust, and 0 per cent verification,' says the entrepreneur with a smile. One RWA member coordinated with iD Fresh and placed the order through WhatsApp or a call. Once the vans delivered the products, the member informed the residents, who would come to collect the products and pay at their convenience through e-wallets. 'Nobody calls them for payment. Nobody knows how much each of them bought. We just trust them,' says Musthafa.

The implicit trust and, with it, the business model, seems to be working. Explains one of the staff members, 'iD Fresh had clocked sales of ₹50 lakh from such Trust Shops in Mumbai in those few months. Amazingly, only 3 per cent of the customers did not pay up.'

The maths, says Musthafa, worked out brilliantly. Had the company sold the same quantity through traditional retail outlets, the collections would have been lower by ₹10 lakh due to retail commissions and wastage. Aided by the pandemic's tailwinds, the company clocked its best monthly sales in September 2020 at ₹24.2 crore. The secret recipe? Trust.

'At some of the retail shops in Bengaluru, Chennai, Hyderabad and Mumbai, where we had these shops, customers deposited fake currency coins, even Monopoly coins, to pick up products. But we persisted. Soon, we got better results. Emotions work. Indians are trustworthy,' Musthafa adds with a disarming smile. Trust begets trust is the insight that Musthafa understood. 'So far, consumers were asked to trust brands, and now brands need to trust consumers. The best way for someone to trust you is to trust them.'

A brand that wants to remain relevant and successful continues to listen to customers and find pain points. Look at how iD Fresh Food made cooking vadas easy for a housewife or any bachelor wanting to try the crispy snack at home. The hardest part of making a medu vada is the hole. From this simple insight came iD's viral product—the Squeeze & Fry Vada Batter. It comes in an umbrella-mechanism-inspired pack that automatically creates the hole as you squeeze the batter into the oil. No hand-wetting or shaping needed!

The most recent innovation from the brand is the launch of the iD Butter Stick. Inspired by the glue-stick design, the iD Twist & Spread Butter Stick packs in 50 grams of fresh, preservative-free butter in such a form that it softens quickly at room temperature. Spreading butter on toast doesn't have to be a tedious, painful task any more! And once you finish your pack, you can simply buy a refill. Says Musthafa:

> Our vada packet, or even the pour-to-perfection coffee liquid bottle, has been highly appreciated and accepted by the consumers at large. Now, with the Twist & Spread Butter Stick, we want to make spreading butter easy. With a unique design, similar to that of a glue stick, consumers no longer have to worry about the butter being too hard or difficult to scrape with a butter knife. Rather, with just a twist, you'll have your butter at room temperature, all ready to spread. We have always taken our consumer's feedback very seriously and, based on that, we were very keen to try something new in the Indian market.

Listening to customers has helped iD innovate continuously. Musthafa elaborates, 'Innovation is all about breaking new ground. When a brand introduces something truly original, it doesn't just spark conversations—it positions itself as a pioneer, securing a lasting edge in the consumer's perception.'

Our discussion with the founder of iD Fresh Food has provided valuable insights into the brand's remarkable journey. Its success is a testament to a strategic blend of innovation, customer-centricity and an unwavering commitment to authenticity. iD Fresh identified a significant gap in the market for fresh, ready-to-cook products that deliver the authentic taste of homemade food without the inconvenience of traditional preparation. Its flagship product, idli and dosa batter, effectively catered to urban consumers seeking both convenience and uncompromised quality.

A key differentiator for iD Fresh has been its dedication to offering 100-per-cent-natural products, free from preservatives, chemicals or artificial additives—aligning perfectly with the growing consumer demand for clean-label food options. By adhering to traditional recipes and using high-quality ingredients, the brand ensures that its products retain the authentic taste and texture of home-cooked meals.

iD Fresh's branding and packaging reflect its core values of simplicity, transparency and natural goodness, reinforcing consumer trust. The brand's emphasis on emotional connections, positioning itself as a facilitator of shared culinary experiences, has further strengthened its appeal. A prime example of its innovative approach is the introduction of the Squeeze & Fry Vada Batter, which redefined home cooking by making the preparation of vadas effortless without compromising tradition.

Recognizing the time constraints faced by urban consumers, particularly working professionals and nuclear families, iD Fresh has consistently tailored its offerings to align with evolving lifestyles. The brand actively engages with its customers, incorporating feedback to enhance product quality and ensure satisfaction. Furthermore, its investment in a robust cold chain infrastructure guarantees product freshness and consistency, reinforcing its reputation for excellence.

The success of iD Fresh lies in its ability to seamlessly merge authenticity, convenience and trust while maintaining a strong focus on quality and innovation. By identifying an unmet consumer need and delivering products that resonate both emotionally and functionally, iD Fresh has carved a distinct niche in the ready-to-cook food segment, setting new industry benchmarks.

iD Fresh batter continues to capture more markets, expanding overseas into the UAE, where a sizable chunk of the Indian population resides.

20

KANAN DEVAN TEA: BRANDING THE SOURCE

Making a brand out of a commodity requires long-term vision, planning, conviction and the right communication. Most commodities, as we saw in the case of atta, are still less than 20 per cent of the market when it comes to branded products. For certain other products, the preparation of the end product is also different, market to market, thus making it difficult for the brand to provide the same experience everywhere. Tea is one such commodity.

'Despite brands being around for nearly a century, tea in loose form holds nearly 70 per cent of the market,' says a senior market researcher from the tea industry. The journey of Kanan Devan Tea—which saw the transformation of a tea garden into a recognized brand and the elevation of a simple commodity into a household name—is nothing short of remarkable.

Normally, tea leaves are bought at auctions. Whether Brooke Bond or Lipton, there is a gap in time between the buying of the tea and its sale to the end consumer. Kanan Devan was sold as loose tea for the longest time. It was faceless, in the sense that it was sold in wooden boxes which one sees at a wholesaler's shop. This was the challenge the brand faced—they needed to convert a staid commodity like tea into a branded entity. It was not an easy problem to solve.

We meet Prabhat Pani at the Bharatiya Vidya Bhavan's S.P. Jain Institute of Management & Research (SPJIMR) campus, where he holds a senior administrative position after retiring from corporate life. He recalls his journey:

> I joined Kanan Devan in the middle of 1983 as a young Tata Administrative Services officer. Kanan Devan were selling loose tea, more as a commodity, while at that time Brooke Bond and Lipton were selling in retail, as branded tea. It was just incidental that in 1985, Krishna Kumar, the then MD, called me and asked me for ideas to increase sale and reduce the commodity contribution. The prices of commodities, tea in this case, fluctuated a lot, and the price going up was not good as there was an agricultural income tax in Kerala which the company wanted to avoid. Darbari Seth, the chairman, wanted to find a way to avoid the fluctuation.

He continues, '"Shall we come out with branded tea?" I suggested to the MD. To my surprise, he agreed. And I was asked to go ahead and formulate a strategy to launch branded tea!'

Prabhat tells us about the situation prevalent then: 'Kerala was a big market and there were smaller markets in the south. There were C&F [carrying and forwarding] agents and, in Kerala, there were two large distributors. The organization was geared to sell commodities. Loose-tea sales constituted 80 per cent of the market, and all the packaged tea sold belonged mainly to Brooke Bond and Lipton.'

He continues, 'There were a few Nilgiri brands. Hyderabad had Lamsa Tea, which was chocolate-flavoured. It was clear that the market had to be captured from loose tea. I worked out a plan to make the change.'

Prabhat and his team did some research to understand why people were buying loose tea. The big insight was about freshness being defined two ways—one was the whiff of flavour which denoted that the tea was coming directly from the plantation, as it was fresher, and the other was that packaged tea was packed in paper packets, which absorbed other smells and thus was not considered fresh enough to be consumed. Some tea paper packets would absorb the smell from the masala packets kept alongside them in the shop, making the tea not at all attractive to customers. Loose tea, therefore, continued to be the choice for a large majority of people.

The proposition was then to keep the freshness intact and the pricing somewhat close to that of loose tea. The other fact to consider was that a loose-tea buyer would buy from a loose-tea seller. So the challenge was to put the final product in the loose-tea outlet. Hence, the positioning of Kanan Devan was 'loose tea in a packet'.

This creation of brand awareness was done in stages. In the first stage, the branding was done on loose tea to convey freshness and make Kanan Devan stand out. Explains ad guru Bharat Dabholkar, who worked on the campaign:

> All wooden boxes are similar: dust, double dust, orange pekoe, and so on. The seller scoops the tea out of the box and gives it to the buyer. We just printed a green stripe on the Kanan Devan box. In Tamil, it was called 'pachai box', meaning green box. We converted the seller into a spokesperson who said the green-striped box was the best. The campaign focused on the stockist talking about it as he is respected by the buyer. In the purchase of loose tea, the buyer is facing the seller and not seeing the box.

Meanwhile, Prabhat went to the Indian Institute of Packaging in Mumbai and, there, he came to the decision of using laminates, which were used by coffee sellers but were not popular elsewhere. He found a polyethylene and low-density polyethylene (LDPE) combination. Polyethylene kept the smell out while the plastic was moisture-proof. A small, newly-set-up unit was willing to do the R&D and trials.

Once the packaging was considered, the next step was to make sure the product was packed at the plantation itself. The proposition was to show that since the tea was packed in the planation, at the source, it was automatically viewed as fresh.

Rather than set up a conventional distribution system, the task was to convert the sellers of loose tea to sell packaged tea. The initial trial was an uphill task. 'The seller of loose tea was not willing to sell packaged tea as he liked the whole concept of being in control, being an adviser to the buyer,' explains Bharat, who studied the seller behaviour.

'Our job was to convince the sellers that if they were selling 100 packets of tea earlier, they would now be selling more. It took us a long time, but the experiment worked,' says Prabhat, who went out into the market to educate the sellers. It was a long, slow journey but it had started showing results.

Says Bharat, 'We launched a plastic pouch with the green stripe to sell the packaged tea. The essence was the green stripe, which transformed Kanan Devan loose tea into a brand getting into retail.'

A marketer with a vision is patient and is willing to let things happen without rushing into simply creating a brand. Kanan Devan is a fine example of that—understanding both customer and buyer behaviour along with seller insights.

Prabhat and Bharat gained insights while travelling around. They knew that the tea is bought at tea auctions in places like Kolkata and Kochi, from where it goes to the packaging centre. They zeroed in on the messaging: 'Kanan Devan is straight from the tea garden, from the plantation to your teacup.'

Bharat says, 'We created a line, "Prakruti oda mishranam, Tata oda packing", which meant that the blending was being done by nature and Tata was merely packing the tea. This was an essential difference between other teas and Kanan Devan. We focused on our strength, which resonated with the customer's inclination of wanting fresh tea.' Bharat further elaborates:

> When Scotch whiskey was getting competition from Suntory of Japan, they created a campaign which emphasized on how nothing can be called Scotch unless it has been produced in Scotland. It is the same case with champagne, which originated in the Champagne region of France. We replicated this strategy for Munnar—that nature has created the perfect situation, the right amount of rain, moisture and sunlight, for the perfect tea. It was the film star Mohanlal's first modelling assignment. In the ad, like in the movie *Mackenna's Gold*, where the sunlight in the morning falls exactly on the opening of the mountain, we created a similar feel in our advertisement where, in God's own country, Kerala, the best tea can be found by leaving at dawn. The travellers then follow the sunlight and reach Munnar to see the Kanan Devan garden. They are amazed at the beauty of the plantation. The message was clear: Kanan Devan tea comes from plantations; hence, it is the freshest.

In another ad, Bharat used the famous runner P.T. Usha, who had received much fame in the Olympics and was known as the Payyoli Express. The idea was to draw an analogy between P.T. Usha's speed and the fast delivery of tea from the tea estate to one's drawing room. In the ad, she is shown running from the tea gardens, through the city streets and to the family which has assembled for breakfast. She throws the Kanan Devan tea packet into the kitchen just in time for the family to enjoy their morning cuppa.

Prabhat says, 'We had a lot of competition in Kerala. Every tea started showing their plantations after we did.'

We ask Bharat how they tackled this perception—that all brands were essentially sourcing from a plantation. What would make Kanan Devan any different?

Bharat explains that they used a series of ads where they tried to show that all teas may come from plantations, which may be as far off as Assam, and showed why Kanan Devan was different. They highlighted the uniqueness of the product.

He says, 'We had ads which compared different products and the gold standard among them. For example, we said: Silks are silks, but Kanjivarams are different. Birds are birds, but the macaw is different. Cars are cars, but the Ferrari is different. And finally, tea is tea, but there is a Kanan Devan difference!'

'The idea was to show that all plantations are not the same, and that ours is very different,' Prabhat adds.

And the ads worked.

Another insight was about how a lot of Malayalis in the Middle East, especially in Dubai, drink tea. There were ads specifically made to target that segment. Explains Bharat, 'In the ad, Mohanlal goes to Dubai and is offered tea. He says that he drinks only Kanan Devan. The family smiles and reply that they too drink Kanan Devan!'

The ad appealed to the NRI market. 'Likewise, we did different ads for every target segment,' adds Bharat.

A lot of focus groups were conducted to understand buyer behaviour. This helped to design the communication. In one such ad, Bharat explains how they failed when they had not taken the local cultural insight into account.

'In one particular ad, Mohanlal plays a schoolteacher. He is the typical husband, the wife presumes, when he seemingly doesn't remember her birthday. When Mohanlal picks her up and takes her home hurriedly, she is disappointed that he doesn't wish her. But when they reach home she is surprised to find that the place is ready and decked up. And Mohanlal brings her Kanan Devan chai as a celebration.'

Bharat chuckles when he says the ad was rejected as Malayali men are not considered so romantic and, hence, women would not like it if their husbands performed such gestures. It went against the local culture. They had to come up with another ad. He elaborates, 'To continue on the theme of freshness, Kanan Devan came up with lines like "Nature works day and night to create the best tea in the world". There were shots of the sunrise, moonlight and much beautiful imagery. It was all about how Kerala wakes up to Kanan Devan.'

Vispy talks of a lot of quantitative research and focus groups created to understand consumer preferences and needs. He has been doing this for forty years and the insights gained are immense. But it needs a different kind of mindset to glean these insights as they are not always visible upfront. Customers don't articulate their preferences the way the brand manager wants to hear them. Kanan Devan and team were willing to listen, rather than prompt the user to articulate their insights. The same product is consumed in different ways in different geographies. While this concept is now common to many food products, it was Kanan Devan who understood it a long time ago. Prabhat explains:

> A significant insight was product formulation. We used this learning but our competition dismissed it as a gimmick. We knew from our research that it was important. The market insight was that the same grain size was not used in all geographies. Homes were a close-enough replication of what was happening at a local tea shop. They learn how to brew their tea from the way they make it in the tea shops. For example, in Kerala, the water is boiled and poured through a long cloth strainer which is full of tea. The time of contact is small, thus they used muslin cloth and fine tea powder. In Tamil Nadu, on the other hand, they use a slightly bigger grain size as the cloth is kept inside the boiling water for a little more time. So it was super-fine dust in Kerala and fine dust in Tamil Nadu, whereas red dust was used in Karnataka.

Branding and pricing were kept constant but the grain size was changed. Kanan Devan was the first one to do such blending, which many brands have now copied. What kind of teas go into a particular geography are based on the form of manufacturing and the kind of milk used. Gujarat and Punjab have a high proportion of milk. The tea needed there is strong. Likewise, a different kind of tea was blended for Maharashtra and Madhya Pradesh.

Prabhat explains the space that tea occupies in the consumer's mind: 'Tea has primarily two dimensions—strength and flavour. We have to find way to tell the story of strength and flavour in different ways. It is creativity which makes the difference.' He continues:

> The colour red is associated with strength and green with flavour. This is set in the consumer's mind. There has to be some way to show either of these attributes. It is not easy to change perceptions. Just because you are creative, you cannot move away from the realm. A third parameter of the brand could be that it makes more cups of tea. But we have to play within these boundaries.

As part of their relaunch campaign in 2021, Kanan Devan showcased the unique diversity of Kerala with a new TV commercial. It was a play on words. Some words mean something totally different in other dialects. This was unique to Malayalam and instils pride in a Malayali. The Kanan Devan campaign is based on this central insight and celebrates the fact that it takes someone who belongs to Kerala to understand this unique diversity of the state. Plunging into this dialect confusion, the campaign picks the right words that cause the confusing situations. To add the quintessential element of authenticity to the story, the scenes in the film are shot at locations where the dialects are commonly used, like Palakkad, Thrissur and Kasargod. Director V.K. Prakash, a Malayali himself, created the films.

Speaking about the campaign, Garima Khandelwal, chief creative officer, Mullen Lintas, says:

> The brand communication with this commercial evolves from the brand being homegrown in Kerala to being homegrown

> to know Kerala like no other. That the dialect in Kerala is so different in different regions that words in the same language are misunderstood was a unique and fresh idea. What is special in this montage is the mix in the casting, to have famous, recognizable artists, who are popularly known to be from the same regions as depicted for the commercial, lend the campaign scale and memorability.[1]

Commenting on the brand restage, Puneet Das, president, packaged beverages, Tata Consumer Products, states:

> Tata Tea Kanan Devan, because of its origin from Kerala's very own Kanan Devan Hills, enjoys a heritage status in the state. Our goal is to deepen the emotional connect the brand enjoys in the state by celebrating the unique facets of the people of Kerala that instils in them a sense of pride. Kanan Devan's new TV commercial illustrates situations wherein the difference in dialects of Malayalam spoken across the various districts of Kerala leads to confusion. [The] situations depicted are so authentic to Kerala that a brand as ingrained as Kanan Devan in Kerala can understand and appreciate the humour. We are sure you will enjoy these witty situations and will definitely agree to the fact [that] one has to be from Kerala, just like Tata Tea Kanan Devan, to really appreciate this uniqueness.[2]

---

1. 'Kanan Devan Celebrates Unique Diversity of Kerala with New Campaign', Exchange4Media, 16 February 2021, https://www.exchange4media.com/advertising-news/kanan-devan-celebrates-unique-diversity-of-kerala-with-new-campaign-110980. html, accessed on 3 April 2025.
2. Ibid.

The success of Kanan Devan lies in its strategic approach to brand building and customer loyalty. The company undertook the significant challenge of transitioning consumers from loose tea to branded options. As a Tata brand, it benefits from a strong heritage and deep-rooted trust. Its legacy is closely tied to the lush tea gardens of Munnar, reinforcing its authenticity. By effectively marketing its connection to the Kanan Devan Hills, the brand emphasizes the natural purity and superior quality of its tea. Advertising campaigns highlight tradition, purity and refreshment, appealing to both older and younger consumers. Consistent quality and taste have cultivated a loyal customer base, with generations relying on Kanan Devan for their daily tea.

By combining high-quality production, a trusted legacy and effective branding, Kanan Devan has maintained its position as a leading tea brand in India. This is a classic example of building a brand from being a commodity to a retail brand and playing on its unique strengths.

21

LENSKART: CHANGING THE 'FACE' OF INDIA

Like tea, there have been products which have been around for decades. Prescription glasses have been around for a long time, and consumers have seen them as purely a necessity—something they needed to wear to correct their eyesight. Then a brand comes along which disrupts this thought process and changes the landscape of the industry.

In the prescription-wear market, brands did exist and there were local brands which enjoyed a loyal customer base. Then comes along Lenskart, which not only disrupts the category but goes on to become the number-one brand nationwide. It is a story of a promoter seeing an opportunity through a different lens, literally, and going on to create a winner.

~

The challenge was to establish a brand that consumers wouldn't merely see as simply selling more prescription eyewear, but something much more than that—something which was personal and aspirational. That the market was huge, largely undifferentiated, with very few large national-level players was a given. But that is not what excited Peyush Bansal when he thought of the idea of Lenskart. He was not talking of taking market share. He was here to create an entirely new market for the brand.

Peyush is an early riser and hard worker. We meet him on a Saturday at 7 a.m. in the NCR region. He is comfortable talking about his business, though it is quite early in the day. And he is ready with slides and a presentation. He has become a celebrity of sorts, with his appearances on *Shark Tank India*, the TV show. And he is also one of the most admired sharks for his simple, decent and friendly approach. But we are not here to discuss *Shark Tank*, and we quickly get to talking about Lenskart and its business!

Lenskart is the story of how a traditional industry like eyewear was rebranded, and the result was a fashion brand which helped improve the customer's appearance while correcting her vision. It was a challenge no one had undertaken.

It was in 2011 that Peyush and his co-founders, Amit Chaudhary and Sumeet Kapahi, launched Lenskart. But before that, they roped in Santosh Desai to understand what the customer was looking for and what were her deciding factors. The industry was huge and there were already a few national-level players. There were known brands like Titan Eye+, which had been launched in 2007. GKB Opticals, a Kolkata-based company, had been around for nearly five decades, but focused on high-end frames and eyewear, many of which were imported. It had its own loyal customer base.

Santosh's mandate was clear: Get consumer understanding on what eyewear meant. Research showed that the entire industry was seen as being an optician and that glasses were a technical product. There were favoured opticians in each city, who had a loyal clientele. A visit to the shop was essentially for vision correction, while some fashion-conscious customers went to stores like GKB which sold imported frames made by Ray-Ban, Dolce & Gabbana, Versace, and so on.

Explains Santosh:

> There was a cultural issue of eyewear being considered more of an essential item to be worn out of necessity, rather than a piece of fashion. It had an element of embarrassment. In many towns, especially in the B and C categories, research showed that a girl with spectacles was not considered beautiful. The common word to describe her would be 'chashmish', denoting someone with glasses. And movies only highlighted this stereotype by featuring professors or lawyers wearing spectacles. Customers remembered Jeetendra, the Jumping Jack hero, transform himself in the movie *Khushboo*. He played the role of Dr Brindaban, and the spectacles are a part of his makeover. Thick glasses were typically associated with someone who wanted a 'professorial look'. A person wearing glasses was considered 'studious'.

Today, Lenskart has changed all that. Eyewear is less of a burden and more of a style statement—there are even some who wear spectacles without power as it adds to their 'aesthetic'. 'In fact, one of most sought-after frames are the round retro ones, or the "Gandhiji look"', a Lenskart store manager in Bengaluru tells us.

But back to research. Consumer feedback showed that the customer was reluctant to change. This disinclination for trying new things can be seen in Bollywood too. Amitabh Bachchan, for example, kept the same hairstyle in movie after movie, and his character was named 'Vijay' in many of his films. Dev Anand was also known for his consistency in style, and this resonated with the customer behaviour and thought process. Status quo was comfortable.

Even in eyewear, the customer had not experimented with style and therein lay the opportunity. She was happy with what she had. She probably had never been shown options. This was an area for Lenskart to work on.

Santosh elaborates:

> There was a huge scope to play around with identity—to challenge the static identity. There was a first-mover advantage of 'playing with the face', and to make the spectacles and eyewear actual identity. The customer was being given a chance to try out a variety of styles and see how she looked as she stood in front of a mirror.
>
> Eyewear was always about vision, being able to 'see better', but Lenskart had showed her that she could also 'look better'. How the spectacles 'looked on me' was the behavioural change Lenskart wanted to introduce.

Santosh explains that the entire market and the consumer insight gleaned was about exploring what 'identity' meant. At the very outset, using these insights, Lenskart became a play on variety and fun. The choices offered were staggering, and the customer had a chance to try out scores of different eyewear styles. The quality of the lenses, ensuring perfection while making the right kind of glasses and all the other technical aspects had not been compromised on either. Now, the customer was trying out the eyewear first to see how she looked, while the optometrist was busy preparing the right kind of lens for them.

Earlier, it was only in the case of sunglasses that the style element was taken into consideration. Lenskart had taken on the task of changing the consumer mindset by introducing face styling as an essential part of purchasing eyewear, be it sunglasses or prescription glasses.

Peyush was clear from day one that he wanted to build a billion-dollar brand and that it was going to happen by changing the game. He says:

> The insights we gathered from the market was what made us stand out from day one. We were driven by purpose, and

> that was about changing the way Indians looked at myopia. We realized that nearly 50 per cent of people suffering from myopia were not using prescription glasses. Unlike in Europe, where an optometrist is available for every 5,000 people or so, in India, it was one for every 50,000 people or more.
>
> There was an element of a 'clinic-like' feel when one went to an optometrist. There is a man wearing a white lab coat, one is asked to fill out a form, and such. It made the customer feel like he was visiting a doctor. We wanted to capture the 'cool' factor of entering a shop to try on spectacles as they looked good on you. The insight we got was about how customers perceived a shop. There was ignorance coupled with the fact that unless the prescription was high, there was no need for glasses to correct vision.

'We played on the technology aspect from day one, and the whole idea was to make it not just easy but fun for the customer. "Select the frame, choose your power and done!"' adds Peyush. No one in this category had built an app for eyewear yet, but Peyush says he believed that was the future.

He continues, 'The whole aspect of "buy two for the price of one" was to allow the customer to change her face whenever she felt like it.' He elaborates:

> We started the concept of 'first frame free' as we wanted the customer to try the frames to begin with. We can only do this because we know that once you try us, you'll love your new glasses and the feel-good factor a stylish new pair of frames bring. And that you'll want to return to the shop, and purchase from us again and again! It was a bold decision to introduce the 'gold membership' programme. Our board members, investors and many others were against it as we were spending a lot of money giving away a second frame free to the customer. But I believed in the idea. The concept of a loyalty programme

in eyewear didn't exist then. We created the category, and it has been a huge success.

Another idea to break the consumer's resistance to trying new frames was allowing them to try the frames at home. Says Peyush:

> Lenskart sends a person home, free of cost, with a huge variety of frames for the customer to try. The glasses too are delivered home. Lenskart Pro Membership is available on Home-Try-On services in India. Through the membership, Lenskart aims to reach new users across 100-plus cities in India, including providing the first piece of eyewear for free from its curated collection of 200-plus prescription glasses (free and anti-glare glasses) and sunglasses.

The Indian customer is never satisfied with just one option. We see ladies in saree shops asking for more colours, more designs, even if they like the saree or dress they have in hand. This is a customer behaviour Lenskart understood well. There are exceptions, of course. When it comes to food products, less is more—a strategy some retail chains follow. The more choice the customer has, the more confused she gets. But we are digressing. We listen to Peyush as he explains, 'Catering to the Indian sentiment of "aur dikhao", we have over 5,000 styles of frames and over forty-five types of lenses. We don't just offer reading glasses but also a range of the latest designer sunglasses.' Such initiatives helped Lenskart greatly to not just overcome inertia but also create a loyal set of customers. Says Ramneek Khurana, co-founder:[1]

1. 'Lenskart aims for 10mn customers with its new Lenskart Pro Membership program', Media Brief, https://mediabrief. com/lenskart-aims-for-10mn-customers-pro-membership-program, accessed on 3 April 2025.

> Lenskart is known for its innovative retailing and technology, which it has used to its advantage for disrupting the eyewear space, first in India and now globally. We constantly try to be technologically advanced yet easy to access for all our customers. We have witnessed more than 50 per cent of sales coming directly from the members as they tend to buy at 4x on repeat, which is more than any other eyewear consumer.

The entire idea of Lenskart was based on consumer research, and they were able to launch something which was a counterpoint to the existing category.

Peyush believes in researching by walking around. Many of his ideas were not approved by the board or his colleagues, but he believes in keeping an ear to the ground and listening to what the customer in the shop is saying. 'I check what my teenage daughter is listening to on YouTube. It is so different from what we may be perceiving as entertainment,' he explains.

He had a lot of objections to his initial ads which were seen as 'frivolous', but Peyush was convinced that the 'cool factor' would soon be a major differentiator. 'We encourage customers to "try" and not necessarily "buy". And that has made a huge difference.' The market is huge, and growing.

An industry consultant who didn't want to be named says, 'While spectacles dominate the total eyewear market in India, the market for sunglasses is growing fastest within the category at a CAGR [compounded annual growth rate] of over 10 per cent for the 2017–24 period. The eyewear market in India is dominated by the unorganized segment, accounting for nearly 80 per cent of the overall market. However, the organized share of the market is growing at a much-faster pace of over 15 per cent CAGR in the forecast period. This high growth is driven by consumers' increased consciousness regarding image and style—the eyewear is gradually shifting towards being a fashion accessory. With a current size of $7.4 billion, the eyewear market is expected to grow at a CAGR of over 9 per cent to reach $13.6 billion by 2024, driven by strong demographics and growing economy.'

Peyush is clear that he is building an eyewear business, while sunglasses will continue to be a small part of his offering. He is making a long bet, and it has been working so far.

Peyush's approach has been to offer the customer value for money. Research showed that often affordability was associated with the product being 'cheap' or not up to the mark. The cheeky ad where Karan Johar argues with Peyush that a frame costing a mere ₹999 would look 'cheap' and pleads with Peyush to increase the Lenskart frame price to at least ₹80,000 if not ₹1 lakh comes to mind. Peyush goes on to argue, in the ad, that there are no middlemen and that the prices are value for money. 'The ad was initially not accepted by many in the management, but I stuck to it. My objective was to show that we offer great quality and an even better price,' he says.

Peyush has launched another brand, John Jacobs, focusing on a slightly higher price range—yet still less expensive than those offered by multinational brands. Using models like Ranveer Brar, Vijay Varma, Masaba and others who appeal to the younger generation, John Jacobs has tapped into the market of young consumers looking for stylish frames to wear to parties or weddings, if not in their daily lives.

Another category which Lenskart is bullish about is the kids' category. Lenskart has launched the Hooper brand to target schoolchildren. 'A few years ago, if you wore glasses to school, you would be called a nerd. It was definitely not cool. It was not easy to find the perfect pair of glasses for your children. Now, with Hooper, we are transforming the way children see the world. It is a long journey, but we are already seeing success,' Peyush explains.

Hooper reminded Peyush of what some of his employees called a 'childish act'. He elaborates:

> We started sending a Kismi toffee with every dispatch. The customer was pleasantly surprised to find a toffee along

with the glasses she had ordered, and it struck a chord. While many thought we were doing childish things, I believed we were reaching out to the 'child' in the target segment of ours, which is largely between ages twenty-five to thirty-five, the young, office-going crowd. We love to do such crazy things!

We are focused on packaging. We want the customer to have a total experience. I saw in Europe that there is a lot of focus on the packaging. I love to spend time observing how things are in various shops, whether in India or abroad.

Now, Peyush says, with sales of more than ₹3,000 crore in 2023 for Lenskart and nearly ₹1,000 crore for John Jacobs, he has his eyes set on capturing more than 30 per cent of the market. 'I want to capture 50 per cent of Bengaluru and a few other cities soon,' he says. With its foray into many cities in India and other countries, Lenskart is on its way to becoming a global brand.

Lenskart's meteoric rise is no accident. It is the result of bold innovation, strategic foresight and a relentless drive to revolutionize eyewear in India. The brand didn't just sell glasses, it shattered old perceptions and turned prescription eyewear into a style statement. With its first-mover advantage, Lenskart transformed an industry, making eyewear more accessible, affordable and irresistibly fashionable.

What sets Lenskart apart is its seamless omni-channel experience, blurring the lines between online convenience and in-store personalization. Customers can explore and purchase glasses with ease, switching effortlessly between digital and physical touchpoints. Cutting-edge technology elevates the experience: the 3D Try-On feature allows users to see exactly how a frame will look before they buy, while AI-driven recommendations ensure they find the perfect match for their face shape and style.

Behind the scenes, Lenskart's high-tech automated manufacturing ensures precision and cost efficiency, allowing the brand to deliver top-quality lenses at competitive prices. Meanwhile, its bold, fashion-forward advertising campaigns have cemented its identity as a youthful, trendy and aspirational brand—one that speaks directly to the style-conscious millennial and the Gen Z audience.

But Lenskart isn't just about fashion—it's about vision. By actively promoting eye-health awareness and the importance of regular check-ups, the brand is not only selling glasses but shaping a future where clear vision is a priority for all. Lenskart isn't just leading the market, it is redefining what eyewear means in India.

Lenskart is disrupting a category, changing buyer behaviour by addressing the pain points in the eyewear market, such as limited accessibility and high costs. Its focus on technology, customer experience and scalability has made it a leader in the eyewear industry.

22

PURO: THE COMPLETE SALT

Let us look at another brand in a category that is ubiquitous. That the product itself is called 'common' salt is not surprising, for we use it every day. To create a space in this category requires not only an understanding of the gap in the customer's mind but also the ability to take on a giant like Tata—who is synonymous with salt.

A little trivia about salt: Everyone knows about Gandhiji's Dandi March being a protest against salt being taxed by the British. When India attained Independence in 1947, salt was being imported from the United Kingdom and Aden (now a city in Yemen) to meet its domestic requirements. But today, India has not only achieved self-sufficiency in the production of salt to meet its domestic requirements but is also in a position to export its surplus. India is the third-largest salt-producing country in the world after China and the US, with its global annual production being about 307 million tonnes. The growth of the salt industry over the last seventy-five years has been spectacular.[1]

---

1. 'Salt Industry in India', Salt Department of India, https://saltcomindia.gov.in/Pdf/SailentFeatures.pdf, accessed on 3 April 2025.

Tata Salt has done a remarkable job in becoming the leader of the category. Its iodized salt helped remove iodine deficiencies for millions of Indians. But a marketer with his ear to the ground always seeks opportunities where most don't. Puro Salt is one such example. They needed to capture the growing trend of 'health awareness' and realize that salt can play a huge role there. The challenge was to uncover the gap in the mind of the customer and to educate her on the benefits of using another brand, compared to what she has been using forever. Puro salt was a pioneer. Many other brands have jumped on to the bandwagon now, but Puro was the first—and the story entails how the promoter researched the market and came out with the proposition.

It takes deep belief to convert a commodity into a brand. And the conviction Ruchir Modi, the founder of Puro Wellness, had, was amazing. Having spent many years at Torrent Pharma, Ruchir established Puro with the intention of providing healthy alternatives to common products.

We are calling salt a commodity, though the default leader in this category is Tata Salt, which is a branded product. Tata Salt carries an undisputable legacy. It has done more to combat iodine deficiency and goitre than any government initiative. The health ministry and the World Trade Organization had, in the early 1980s, informed the Central government that the only cost-effective way of delivering iodine to the masses was through salt. Anxious to tackle the growing health problem, N.D. Tiwari, the then minister of industry, requested Darbari Seth of Tata Chemicals to take up the cause.

Such was the legacy against the backdrop of which Ruchir had to launch a brand—that too at a higher price point—and convince customers that it was better! It was truly a challenging task.

Ruchir wanted to introduce a healthier version of salt, something Indians had been consuming for time immemorial, but which had not been sold as a brand yet. After all, 'sendha namak', or rock salt, is not new to Indians. Ruchir realized that the product was well-known but had not been introduced into mainstream cooking for some reason. Sendha namak has been traditionally used across various regions and cultures for its culinary, medicinal and religious significance. The term 'sendha' indicates its association with the Sindh region, where rock salt was historically mined and traded by Sindhi merchants. During fasting periods, rock salt is often consumed as it is considered pure and unprocessed, compared to regular table salt. It is used in Ayurvedic recipes as well due to its perceived benefits for digestion and overall health.

'The first thing we did was study salt as a category,' says Priya Lobo, CEO of Ormax, who carried out the research for Darshan Patel, Ruchir's mentor and the founder of Paras Pharma. She says:

> Darshan wanted to know what the role and relationship of salt was in cooking. It was as basic a necessity as cooking oil but used in a much-smaller quantity. The question the researcher wanted to understand was: What does salt to do the food? What are its properties?

This research delved into to the very basics before launching a brand. Quite naturally, the 'saltiness' of salt was very important, and the right quantity made all the difference to the food. In Indian cooking, salt plays a crucial role as a fundamental flavour enhancer, used to balance the complex spice profiles of dishes by bringing out the taste of other ingredients—although it's often added with a lighter hand compared to some other cuisines, with the focus on 'swaad anusaar', meaning as per taste; salt is considered essential but needs to be used carefully to avoid overpowering the dish.

Rock salt did just this—enhance the flavour and taste—and Ruchir believed it was a far healthier version of the ordinary table salt sold by Tata. Even though it was common wisdom that rock salt was healthier, for it contained lots of nutrients and minerals that common salt didn't have, it was sold loose and was more expensive, being used for poojas and religious functions but not as a substitute for white salt in daily cooking.

The other alternative was Himalayan pink salt which is found in the Mandi region in India. But the majority of Himalayan pink salt is imported from Pakistan, specifically from the Khewra Salt Mine located in the Punjab region in the foothills of the Himalayas.

Ruchir wanted to change the cooking habits of Indians to make them switch from ordinary white salt to Puro. He came up with the idea of making pink salt a necessity and a healthy substitute for white salt. This meant taking on a category characterized by high inertia. The default brand and name for salt was Tata Salt. Tata had made their iodized salt a part of the household lingo, and the housewife would be averse to changing this habit so easily.

The detailed market research, which was Darshan bhai's style, continued. The moment of truth came when a cohort of thirty-five- to forty-five-year-old women was asked about the properties of Himalayan pink salt. They said they were looking at healthier alternatives as salt was known for causing high blood pressure and other problems. But they were under the impression that pink salt was less 'salty' and hence not as good as ordinary salt for cooking.

Taste tests showed that pink salt indeed had great saltiness and, in fact, needed to be used in lesser quantities, thus reducing health risks. They also found that a packet of Puro salt lasted for a month and half and longer, while Tata Salt was consumed in lesser time. The price, as we discussed earlier, was a function of the value provided, and clearly the cohort was able to see value in Puro. The high price point of ₹100 was thus not questioned. Further research showed, convincing Ruchir that he was on the right track, that the nutrients in Puro salt were seen by customers as very healthy. Many customers talked of 'feeling light' after a meal made using Puro.

The rock salt sold in the market was available in big globules, while Puro, though not as fine as Tata Salt, was seen perfect to use due to its granularity.

A need had been identified, and a brand was born. The name Puro directly connects with purity. The simplicity of the name makes it easier for the customer to connect with it.

Anil Kapoor, known for his fitness, was chosen as the brand ambassador. In the ad he tells consumers that white salt goes through a bleaching process in a factory, Puro was a natural salt with eighty-four minerals, highlighting how Puro was very different from ordinary salt. In another ad, a group of women assembled for a party ask the host why she uses Puro when 'all of India is using white salt'. She answers saying it is because it's Puro. The friends ask her whether Puro contains iodine, zinc and such. She replies, 'Puro has eighty-four minerals.' The ad clearly positions Puro not only as a healthier salt but a far better substitute to plain white salt for regular cooking.

Puro's remarkable success is a testament to its ability to harness the surging demand for health-focused products through strategic marketing, premium positioning and an unwavering commitment to purity. As consumer awareness around healthy eating continues to grow, Puro has masterfully capitalized on the shift toward unrefined and natural foods. Its branding resonates with urban consumers who are not only conscious of what they consume but are also willing to pay a premium for superior quality and authenticity.

By transforming a commoditized product into a distinguished brand, Puro has carved out a unique space in the market, setting new benchmarks in the industry. Its disruptive impact is evident, forcing even legacy giants like Tata Salt to introduce pink-salt variants in response. While many brands have since followed suit, Puro stands as the pioneer that redefined the category, proving that innovation and vision can turn even the most traditional products into national successes.

The Puro story shows that with the right research and insights, it is possible to enter a commodity which is dominated by a single brand—and make a difference!

CONCLUSION

Establishing market leadership in an undifferentiated product category is not only possible but achievable through holistic thinking. Building a leading brand requires a strategic approach that integrates product, pricing, promotion and packaging—elements that collectively strengthen the brand, making it resilient and difficult to dethrone. Achieving leadership in any category demands a leap of faith, exemplified by success stories in cement, jewellery and packaged flour. The foundation lies in unwavering belief in the product, followed by meticulous planning and systematic execution. Even in a commoditized market, differentiation is possible when a brand has a clear identity and offers a compelling value proposition that resonates with customers.

Creating a successful brand in a price-driven commodity market necessitates strategic differentiation, emotional engagement and innovative positioning. Leading branding and advertising experts agree that brands must go beyond functional benefits to forge an emotional bond with consumers. Those that successfully craft a unique selling and value proposition stand out in the marketplace. As David Ogilvy famously stated, 'Tell the consumer exactly what makes you different—and do it in a memorable way.' Similarly, an ad industry maxim asserts, 'People don't buy what you do; they buy why you do it.'

Marketing thought leaders emphasize the power of community in brand building. Seth Godin encourages entrepreneurs to cultivate a 'tribe' around their brand by fostering meaning and engagement, as seen in Lenskart's success. Jeff Bezos encapsulates the essence of branding with his insight: 'Your brand is what other people say about you when you're not in the room.' Understanding customer perception requires in-depth research and an ability to uncover the insights consumers reveal in the brand's absence.

PART 4

Creating Leaders by Beating Competition

In the world of business, challenging an established market leader—especially one with a near-monopolistic hold—requires not only audacity but a profound understanding of the market and consumer psyche. When it comes to confronting an iconic brand like Iodex, a name that has been around for generations, most marketers would shy away. After all, who dares to challenge a century-old institution? But therein lies the opportunity. This is where true disruptors thrive, ready to flip the script of industry dominance.

Take another monumental challenge: Going head-to-head with a titan like Hindustan Unilever's AXE deodorant. The odds seem insurmountable for a local player, right? Yet, when Darshan Patel set his sights on the painkiller and deodorant markets, few believed he had what it took to dethrone the giants. However, today, his brands aren't just surviving, they're thriving, perched at the pinnacle of their categories, having obliterated competitors and left them in the dust. So what does it take to unseat a reigning champion and claim the top spot? To displace a clear category leader requires more than confidence—it demands a deep understanding of the present landscape. Success doesn't come from simply identifying the leader's weaknesses; it requires a perfect combination of product excellence, strategic positioning and the ability to communicate effectively with the consumer. It's about tapping into their subconscious, understanding their desires and frustrations and delivering a product that meets—and exceeds—expectations.

The tale of David and Goliath from the Bible is a classic example. A mere shepherd boy, armed with no more than a sling, faced the towering Goliath, a giant who seemed invincible. But David had some crucial information—the giant's weakness lay in his forehead. With one perfectly aimed stone, David struck the mighty Goliath, toppling him. The lesson? Knowing where to strike is winning half the battle.

Greek mythology offers another example. Antaeus, the invincible giant, drew strength from his connection to the earth. But when Heracles realized that removing him from the ground would weaken him, he lifted Antaeus high and crushed him. The key to victory? Understanding the source of your competitor's strength and then exploiting it.

The story of Achilles, whose vulnerable heel led to his downfall, is another timeless example of how a seemingly invulnerable opponent can be defeated if you know where to strike. These stories aren't just myths, they're fundamental lessons in competitive strategy. To beat a leader, you must first understand where they're vulnerable.

In business, this means recognizing when a brand leader becomes too comfortable in its dominance. A market leader that has been without true competition for too long risks becoming generic, losing its identity in the process. This is a dangerous, double-edged sword. On the one hand, being the default choice is powerful; on the other, it opens the door for a challenger to redefine the category and make the once-untouchable brand irrelevant.

Consider the example of Dalda, once the undisputed name in vanaspati ghee. As its name became synonymous with the product itself, it slowly slid into the realm of 'generic'—a fate that also befell Xerox, Kleenex and Band-Aid. When a brand becomes synonymous with the product, the real battle begins: How to maintain its distinctiveness? As Vispy puts it, the costs of letting your brand slip into generic status are astronomical, with corrective advertising and re-education campaigns often being necessary to reclaim lost ground.

But some brands evolve, like Thums Up, which adapted to the changing times and maintained its relevance. Beating an established leader doesn't just take courage—it requires knowing exactly where to hit. By understanding what the consumer truly craves and what gaps exist in the current offering, a challenger can focus all its energies on striking that weak spot with precision.

Darshan Patel's journey with Paras Pharma[1] makes the perfect case study. Armed with a deep understanding of the market and an unshakable belief in his brand's potential, Patel launched Moov, a painkiller that quickly surged to leadership status. The story of Moov's rise is a testament to the power of insight, strategy and execution—the very qualities that can propel a challenger from obscurity to dominance.

---

1. Paras Pharma was sold to Reckitt Benckiser in 2010. Some brands were later bought by Marico, but these owner changes are not relevant to the brand story and the brands which were created by Darshan Patel and later taken forward by the respective owners.

23

MOOV: DISLODGING A 100-YEAR-OLD COMPETITOR

Moov had a clear challenge—that of dislodging a competitor who had been around for more than a century. The market was attractive as it was underserved, despite its competitor being around for such a long time. There were local pain-relieving balms and some age-old remedies like Tiger Balm, which originated in Rangoon, Burma (now Yangon, Myanmar), in the late nineteenth century. Clearly, as tempting as it was to get into the category, it needed thorough research to position the brand clearly in the minds of the consumer. Vispy, who has worked with Darshan Patel of Paras Pharma for decades, explains:

> Before we talk about Moov, let us understand the category of external painkillers, typically found in balms. According to the WHO's Global Burden of Disease study, one in every fifth person is likely to be suffering from pain, with muscular pain being a frequent condition that can hamper one's spirit and

> prevent them from going that extra mile in life. When it came to external pain relief, sprains and other aches in India, Iodex was the default brand that a consumer reached out to. It has been around for a very long time.

Vispy has conducted studies for the pain-relief market, which, he says, is 'significant'. As per an estimate, it was in the range of ₹4,500 to ₹5,000 crores in 2022.[1]

At times, the easiest way to dislodge a leader is to identify its weaknesses and then create a product addressing them. That is what Moov did. And simplistic as it sounds, it made Moov the clear leader in the category of pain relief. Most over-the-counter or OTC products of this kind have ingredients like diclofenac, methyl salicylate, and such. Iodex, a product of GlaxoSmithKline, is more than a century-old brand and was identified as the product to use when one had aches, pains and sprains. With one hundred years of heritage, Iodex was clearly the leader. To take its position needed some clear thinking, simple yet effective strategies and a belief that the brand was clearly addressing the gaps.

A random study of medical stores done by Vispy and his team highlighted customer preferences. Zandu Balm, Tiger Balm and Amrutanjan are all associated with providing relief against headache, cold and body ache due to fever. In fact, Zandu, launched by Zandu Pharma and later acquired by Emami, usurped Amrutanjan, which had been around for more than a century. Again, this was a case of a product leader's space taken up by an upstart!

We visit a medicine shop to observe what the customer asks for when she is looking for a pain reliever. The answer is clear—it is

---

1. 'RB to expand market share in pain relief segment', *The Economic Times*, last updated 26 September 2019, https://economictimes. indiatimes. com/industry/cons-products/fmcg/rb-to-expand-market-share-in-pain-relief-segment/articleshow/71315741.cms?from=mdr, accessed on 4 April 2025.

Moov! When the shopkeeper was quizzed about whether people ask for it by its brand name, the answer is a clear yes. Moov is the default pain-relieving gel that customers go for. The new entrant was able to topple a veteran by understanding the weaknesses of the leader and targeting it with precision.

Explains Vispy about how Darshan Patel came up with the idea behind Moov:

> The generic 'Ooh, Aah, Ouch!' of Iodex was an excellent line but it didn't convey any specific usage. Most customers also didn't like the stain it left behind either, because of its disgusting black colour, as well as its repulsive smell! That it was in a glass bottle which needed to be scooped out was another problem.

During our research, we found, much to our surprise, a 1925 advertisement of Iodex claiming to be 'non-staining, non-irritating Iodine'. It is also shown as being excellent for rheumatism, swollen glands, ringworm, acne, eczema and other inflammatory diseases!

Iodex was so popular that it was almost generic. And while this was clearly one of its strengths, it was also a chink in the armour for Moov to penetrate.

Communication is a key element of any product launch, and in Moov's case it was implemented from day one. It begins with the name. 'Iodex' doesn't tell a customer that it is a pain-relieving ointment but Moov makes it clear: 'It makes you *move*!' It was the product positioning in the communication and its usage which worked for Moov.

Explains Darshan bhai, 'We are not talking about all kinds of pain—like a stomach ache. Neither are we generically talking about aches and hurts. If your elbow hurts or your ankle is sprained, you may use Iodex. But when your back or your waist is hurting, you use Moov.' Vispy elaborates:

> The positioning of Iodex was as a specialist for sprains and strains. But for everything else, there is Moov! Most readers won't remember the last time they had an ankle sprain but would recall the last time they had a backache. This is where Moov positioned itself. If it was an ankle sprain, one may use Iodex, but the Moov advertisement focused on backache—the lower back, specifically.

He continues, 'The message to the woman was, "If your back is hurting, use Moov."' It was a well-thought-through and deliberate communication strategy, positioning the product for backache, knowing that more people would remember the brand and reach out for the product when their backs hurt.

Says Darshan Patel, 'After all, when an ankle is sprained, one may use a little bit of Iodex. But the back needs a large amount of the balm. Suddenly, the consumption dramatically increased. Not only did the communication help the brand position itself, but it increased the usage.'

The idea of moving the product to the bedroom was another part of the communication strategy. At home, one may find a few tablets, Burnol, Iodex, etc., in the medicine box. But not Moov—because it is usually kept on the bedside table or in the drawer, within arm's reach. It is the first choice for pain relief.

It was all about repositioning the product, along with constant communication. To compete with the leader, Iodex, in this case, Moov thought differently. And a study of its advertisements shows how well the brand has succeeded.

A housewife suffers from backache, and her loving husband rubs the ointment on her back. The name Moov also makes it clear. 'Aah se aaha tak!' was their tagline. Simple, straightforward, effective.

The communication strategy was based on consumer research. Chennai has a huge water problem. And when women and families are lifting buckets of water, a backache is the expected outcome.

And Moov comes straight to the point to address this problem. The advertisement speaks to the target segment clearly. They, the women, know Moov is their solution.

A big brand like Moov is created from well-defined needs, and by communicating well-defined problems and solutions for these needs.

Today, the market has many pain-relief sprays, but the touch which an ointment provides is missing. The product is not just about its effectiveness but about the loving touch which adds to the relief. Vispy explains the emotion of a loving touch:

> Vicks has used this concept of 'touch' extremely well. Vicks is all about the emotions of touch and love. It has made an entire empire out of this. It is all about the touch of the loving mother, the doting wife—touching her husband's or child's chest or forehead when they're unwell.
>
> Vicks is not selling a solution for a cold but it talks about love—tender mother's love. The thinking behind Vicks is about mother's love and how the child recovers after she puts Vicks on her child's chest.

He elaborates on the strategy used by Moov. 'In India, most times, it is the sister or mother who applies the pain balm. It is not the husband. Moov broke the stereotype by getting the husband to apply the ointment for his wife suffering from lower back pain.'

The classic positioning of the product on the bedside table is a simple yet effective way of not only increasing usage but ensuring recall. These insights were gained through extensive market research. The communication based on the research ensured that the brand was never in the medicine cabinet. Getting men to apply it on their wives and keeping the tube by the bedside were two important ingredients in the communication strategy that worked for Moov.

When a medical shop owner is asked about a solution for headaches, he talks about Tiger Balm, Amrutanjan and now Zandu Balm. They are clear leaders. But when it comes to joint pains, it is Moov and nothing else!

For Paras Pharma, the company that owned Moov (before Paras was sold to Reckitt Benckiser), it was easy to launch the brand as the company was earlier selling Stopache—a product sold through retail pharmacies. The first port of call was the pharmacy shops.

All elements of marketing were considered. For example, the packaging of Moov is quite ordinary. Moov's promoters believed that the customer takes the tube out of the pack and throws it away. Spending money on attractive packaging was considered money not used well. And the idea seems to have worked.

Moov has built leadership based on a simple and straightforward communication strategy which was derived from consumer insights.

Moov's success lies in its ability to empathize with consumer pain-points, innovate its product offerings and establish a trusted, recognizable brand identity. By focusing on back-pain relief, connecting emotionally with its audience and maintaining affordability and accessibility, Moov has sustained its leadership in the pain-relief category. Moov differentiated itself by focusing specifically on backaches, which is a common issue in India due to sedentary lifestyles, heavy manual work and a lack of ergonomic awareness. This niche focus allowed Moov to stand out in a market crowded with generic pain-relief products.

> *The empathy the ads showed for women created a strong emotional connect with the consumer. Moov's advertising campaigns often highlighted the challenges faced by women managing household chores and work-related stress, resonating deeply with its target audience. A simple and direct name recall and relentless advertising has made the brand strong—all the elements have come together to allow Moov to not just move Iodex but literally dislodge it from its shelf space.*

Moov's leadership position continues till today, with Reckitt Benckiser.

24

FOGG: ALL PERFUME, NO GAS

For a tropical country like India, it is natural that people use deodorants. It is a huge market, according to one industry observer, to the tune of a few thousand crores, though he didn't quote exact numbers. (As per some reports it is around ₹4000 crore.[1]) No doubt, it is tempting for a business to enter a market of this size, but the challenge comes when one is tackling one very large established player in the category. In this case, it was Hindustan Unilever with its brand AXE, which has been around since 1999. (ITC, another giant, introduced Engage deodorants late in 2013.)

It was this challenge that Vini Cosmetics decided to tackle head-on. Just like we saw in the case of Moov, it all was about beating a market giant like Hindustan Unilever with a simple concept which exposed the weakness of the brand AXE. Says Vispy, 'They were not just targeting AXE but the entire deodorant market.'

---

1. 'Deodorants: India', Statista, https://www.statista.com/outlook/cmo/beauty-personal-care/personal-care/deodorants/india, accessed on 4 April 2025.

The challenge for Vini Cosmetics, Darshan Patel's new company, after he sold Paras Pharma to Reckitt Benckiser, was about how to create a position in the market which not only allowed the brand to establish itself but questioned the very existence of all the other deodorant brands.[2] The golden rule of all advertising is: Offer real, genuine value. And Fogg did precisely that, showing how it was genuine value for money for the customer.

Let us dig deeper into the story.

~

Darshan Patel was keen to launch a perfume. 'I want a truly Indian perfume; it should be the Titan of Indian perfumes,' he said. There was no genuinely Indian perfume in the market (except attar), and an opportunity arose to bridge the gap. The year was 2011.

Research was done by Vispy and his team to understand how Indians used perfume, and whether the concept of 'perfume' was understood at all. The findings showed that customers understood what was loosely called 'scent', and it was mainly used by aunties and mothers. Most men didn't use perfume, and while there was some usage of attar (or itr) among the Muslim community, the segment was just not big enough. And it was managed by local vendors or traditional perfume sellers. For instance, we see some of them in the Chandni Chowk area of Delhi, and they have been around, as they claim, since Mughal times.

Coming back to the research done by Ormax and team, the findings showed that the Indian male equated deodorants with perfume. The opportunity thus lay in not launching a perfume but in a deodorant spray. AXE, from Hindustan Unilever, was the undisputed leader in that category. The ad showed a man liberally spraying the deodorant on his body and how women drooled all

---

2. As the ad guru David Ogilvy said, 'Consumers still buy products whose advertising promises them value for money, beauty, nutrition, relief from suffering, social status, and so on.'

over him. The market research found a gap—the Indian mind was not forgiving and, while it was familiar with the concept of spraying on perfume, it was correlated, rightly so, with wastage. Deodorant thus stood for wastage. The customer was not sure how much actual deodorant was being sold to him. He felt it was all gas—literally.

The other thing to consider was the AXE deodorant ads. While all of them showed how a man gets women after spraying AXE, the ads were merely seen as humorous—no one really believed that AXE would attract women, and the ads were thus rejected.

Vispy and his team presented their research findings—the benefits to be gained from clear communication. There was a need to directly communicate with the customer about what value was added in this product. The new brand created by Darshan Patel was Fogg, and the ad was clear in its approach.

The advertisement features a customer applying an unnamed deodorant, only to express frustration, saying, 'Phir khatam!' The voiceover follows with the explanation that the product runs out quickly because it contains a significant amount of gas. This is followed by the introduction of Fogg: 'A spray without gas.' The ad then effectively demonstrates the difference between the two products by showcasing how Fogg delivers more liquid when sprayed into a glass tumbler. While the competitor's product fills only a third of the tumbler, Fogg fills more than half, emphasizing its superior value.

By highlighting the value proposition of over 800 sprays per can, Fogg effectively communicated its superior cost-effectiveness. More importantly, the message of 'no gas' resonated deeply with consumers, who associated gas with wastage. Fogg's innovative positioning of 'no gas, no wastage; 800 sprays guaranteed' quickly struck a chord with customers, establishing the brand as a clear leader in the market.

Vispy's market research team had found that while, at the emotional level, the customer found gas to be a waste, the messaging was entirely rational. The communication didn't talk about emotions but showed, in stark contrast, how Fogg was far more value for money.

The ability to convert a pain point (that is 'no perfume, only gas', which meant wastage) to a rational proposition worked. AXE was dislodged from its top spot and Fogg soon became number one. It has stayed at that position since 2011. ITC, with its Engage perfume, is a strong competitor but is still behind Fogg.[3]

To further solidify the brand's dominance and maintain its market ubiquity, Fogg conducted additional research after establishing itself as the clear leader.[4] The research revealed that the popular market phrase among dealers was 'Kya chal raha hai?'—a common inquiry about trending products. To reinforce its positioning as 'India's number-one perfume body spray', Fogg launched a series of advertisements. The ads featured simple yet effective dialogues, with one person asking, 'Kya chal raha hai?' and the response being, 'Aaj kal Fogg chal raha hai.'

The advertisements were presented in various humorous scenarios of different duos engaging in this question-and-answer banter: a doctor asking a patient, an Indian soldier being queried by a Pakistani counterpart across the border and two shopkeepers speaking to each other. These situations reinforced Fogg's leadership position in a relatable and engaging manner.

The voiceover further reinforced the message, urging consumers, shopkeepers and others to make a straightforward choice with the command, 'Sochiye mat!' This approach effectively removed any

---

3. In 2019, Engage was India's number-two deodorant brand, according to Nielsen data, with a hold of nearly 11 per cent of the market share, while Fogg was the market leader with 18 per cent market share in a ₹3,047-crore segment nationally.
4. Udit Mukherjee, 'ITC eyes top position in deo market', *Times of India*, last updated 29 March 2019, http://timesofindia.indiatimes.com/articleshow/68623268.cms?utm_source=contentofinterest&utm_medium=text&utm_campaign=cppst, accessed on 4 April 2025.

hesitation in the minds of the consumers, solidifying Fogg as the unequivocal number-one brand.

Launched just over a decade and a half ago, the story of Fogg offers valuable insights into successful market strategy. Fogg has achieved remarkable success in India's deodorant market through innovative approaches and a keen understanding of consumer needs. Its USP centred around being a 'no gas' deodorant, highlighting liquid content over gaseous propellants. This strategy not only ensured more sprays per bottle but also delivered greater value to consumers, particularly resonating with the value-conscious audience.

Fogg's highly effective marketing campaigns have played a significant role in its success. While the brand's achievements may seem straightforward in retrospect, they are the result of a strong conviction and the promoter's ability to communicate the brand's value proposition consistently and persuasively. This required substantial investment in advertising, driven by the firm belief that such spending would ultimately drive sales and deliver long-term returns.

Keeping the message simple and effective, with hard-hitting ads worked wonders for Fogg, which rules the deodorant market now.

25

THUMS UP: LEFT TO DIE, RISES TO DOMINATE

As we saw earlier, it is extremely difficult to change the habits of customers when it comes to certain food categories. And cold drinks is one such category where consumer loyalties are strong. But when you already have the legacy of being a top seller, but were forced to retreat because of changes in the management, there is much potential here for the phoenix to rise from the ashes.

Thums Up is one such amazing story. It is about beating multinational brands like Pepsi and regaining what was originally its number-one position. Thums Up faced multiple challenges from being relegated to the dustbin to creating a leadership position for itself while being threatened by global brands like Coca-Cola and Pepsi, which were almost generic names for the black fizzy drink.

The Thums Up journey is not just about the right positioning but also about realizing the inherent strength of a brand. It is a story based on consumer research and then using insights gleaned from it to rise from the ashes to the top. A little background here. Thums Up was once the only cola in India (there was Campa Cola as well, predominantly in north India, but it soon vanished in 1991) after Coke was asked by India's then industries minister, George Fernandes, to exit India in 1977. When multinational brands regained entry into India after the opening up of the economy in 1991, giants like Coke and Pepsi were able to re-establish their presence here. In this scenario, in 1993, Coke snapped up Thums Up. The cola wars were ongoing, and with Reliance Industries' recent purchase of another iconic brand, Campa Cola, the war was going to be interesting! But we are not discussing that here.

While today, Thums Up continues to be the largest cola brand (it is now a billion-dollar brand),[1] this was not the case when Coke bought it. 'The move to buy the brands (Gold Spot, Limca and Thums Up) from Parle was to basically kill them and make Coca-Cola the number-one brand,' says Arvind Sharma, ex-CEO of Leo Burnett, the agency which had helped launch Thums Up in 1993. He continues, 'While they were spending ₹200 crore for Coca-Cola, the same amount as PepsiCo was allocating for Pepsi Cola, in 1995, the ad budget for Thums Up was a meagre ₹1.8 crore. That's a ratio even less than 1:100!'

Ramesh Chauhan, the founder and chairman of the Parle Group, and the original cola king of India, who has created Thums Up, along with Limca, Maaza and Gold Spot, still recalls the attempts made by Coke to kill the iconic brand and promote its own:

> We had created these brands to fill the vacuum [following Coke's exit from the India market in 1977]. And we succeeded and did very well. But when I sold Thums Up to Coke, the

---

1. 'Thums Up becomes a billion-dollar brand', *The Economic Times*, 10 February 2022, https://economictimes.indiatimes.com/industry/cons-products/food/thums-up-becomes-a-billion-dollar-brand/articleshow/89486419.cms?from=mdr, accessed on 4 April 2025.

> funny thing is, they didn't appreciate the value of the brand. They actually tried to kill it. That's a bit odd.[2]

Chauhan, who was closely watching the developments after handing over his prized possession to the Atlanta-based cola major in 1993, recalls that at least for the first two years, Coca-Cola did not allocate any budget at all for Thums Up. 'I was watching carefully. I was surprised to see that there was a strong [effort] to underplay Thums Up. They stopped advertising. Soft drinks cannot survive without ads!'[3]

Coke soon discovered that Thums Up had a set of loyal customers and decided to give it a shot. The sales of Thums Up in 1993 were a shade higher than Coke and Pepsi.

An industry veteran adds, 'It was a classic case of Pepsi being squeezed between Thums Up and Coke. But the real victory for Thums Up was the way market insights were used to market the brand and create a position which was unshakeable.'

Arvind Sharma recalls a meeting with the then CEO of Coke in India. The swanky office was then in Mumbai, though later they shifted to Gurugram. He tells us:

> We were not sure what the meeting was for. We presumed it might be a new account for us to look at for brand Coke. But to our surprise, the discussion began about Thums Up! We learnt that the management team was stumped by the customer loyalty for Thums Up. They feared they were killing the golden goose. They decided to give Thums Up a shot. The management team was not sure what exactly they wanted us

---

2. Arnab Dutta, 'Tasting the thunder: How Thums Up rose to become a billion-dollar brand', *Business Today*, 8 March 2022, https://www.businesstoday.in/latest/corporate/story/tasting-the-thunder-how-thums-up-rose-to-become-a-billion-dollar-brand-325041-2022-03-07, accessed on 4 April 2025.

3. Ibid.

> to do. They only told us to revive the brand. The initial launch campaign for Thums Up was managed by the ad agency Trikaya Grey (where the slogan 'Happy Days Are Here Again' was used), which set the brand on its path of growth. The brand was then handled by Ambience, which did the 'Taste the Thunder—Toofani Thanda' campaign. When the brand was acquired by Coke, Ambience was sacked, and the brand languished before Leo Burnett was given the mandate.

Arvind Sharma and his team left the Coke office and huddled in the agency's office. They had to come up with something radically different. It was a particularly hot day as they all sat sipping on Thums Up while trying to brainstorm on the product attributes. Bottles of Coke and Pepsi were kept in the office too. Each one had their own take on what the products stood for.

Sharma found that the earlier ads for Thums Up were no different from other cola brands—that of friends coming together to enjoy their soft drinks. We see, in a 1985 ad, a young Sunil Gavaskar, Ravi Shastri and Sandeep Patil enjoying a game of passing a bottle opener, a bottle of Thums Up and a cricket ball. It was all about food, fun, laughter and Thums Up.

'Most cola wars consisted of screaming the loudest to remain relevant in the consumer's mind,' says an ad veteran. 'If you see Pepsi's 1996 ad, when they lost the official sponsorship for the World Cup, they launched a blitzkrieg to counter Coke's claim of the sponsorship with the tag line, "Nothing official about it". But it doesn't say anything about why a customer should drink Pepsi.'

Arvind adds, 'We realized that Thums Up ads neither differentiated the brand from others nor played on its inherent strength—that of being a strong cola.'

While the team felt that Thums Up was decidedly 'stronger', Sharma commissioned comprehensive research to understand what the customer liked in particular about Thums Up. They wanted to understand why the customer was so loyal to it. They found that the customer could clearly identify Thums Up in a blind taste test because of its distinct, strong fizz, while Pepsi and Coke were largely undifferentiated. The customer liked Thums Up for this characteristic—its strength was its strength!

Says a market researcher and a die-hard fan of Thums Up, laughing, 'The fact that one burped loudly after having Thums Up, despite someone nearby getting irritated, was an indication of its strong fizz. We all loved it! It had a macho image.'

Sharma recalls, 'We brainstormed based on this insight and came up with the idea of re-establishing the brand based on its masculinity factor. The idea was to position it as a larger-than-life, adventure-driven brand that came together as a very compelling package for the eighteen-to-thirty-five-years age group.'

The first series of ads were all about masculinity and physical strength. The ad showed a macho man in a leather jacket on a motorbike, who saves a damsel in distress from goons and then, having done his job, rides off into the sunset.

This worked well for a few years. Thums Up was gaining ground. Coke was happy to see that the brand they wanted to kill was actually doing well.

When Coke re-entered India, it was the 1990s. Now, in the latter half of the decade, India was changing and so was the consumer. Sharma and his team conducted another round of research to understand the changing dynamics and customer understanding. No longer was it necessary to show an angry young man to depict strength. To continue and ensure brand salience, the idea evolved to turn the strength shown from physical to mental.

This is where Vispy and the Ormax team stepped in. Says Agnello Dias of Taproot India, the agency which carried out the work:

> Ormax came in when the ad was written. The soft drink category till that point was about the functional or emotional benefit of having the drink. That way, the message was product functionality. The line was 'Taste the Thunder', but what they

showed was people enjoying Thums Up. There weren't any particular type of persons who drank Thums Up. The notion of new-age machismo, unlike the current ad [back then], where a basketball hoop was set on fire and the alpha male was seen dunking the ball, was not about the angry young man but was more like Shahrukh in *DDLJ*, who makes the parents agree to the relationship rather than eloping with the girl.

The traditional depictions of male machismo included biking and boxing, and so on. Bungee jumping was very new and had not been seen on TV in India all that much. It was a pretty cool act. We weaved the role of the product and the brand into the film. Ormax and Vispy came in to help with the research as we couldn't come up with a storyboard. People would not understand bungee jumping.

It was Vispy's genius that he came up with an unheard-of concept in the research, which was about narrating the entire script to a focus group. We had never done it before and haven't done it since. We narrated the same story the same way to different groups in India. We didn't use the phrase 'bungee jumping' as no one would understand. The idea of the new-age male came in as we were seeing that the classical brawny machismo was not 'cool' any more. The new generation identified with someone who was comfortable with his machismo and didn't need to wear it on his sleeve. He is not an adventurer but does it casually—thus introducing the mock wave with his hand before he jumps down the cliff. The idea of what is cool for the youth was changing. That was the key insight from the research. The image of the strong silent guy at the bar was being phased out by the image of someone who participated and engaged with everyone.

The complexity of the script needed research to understand whether the plotline would gel with the modern generation. 'The last shot of the truck driver finding a bottle missing was to reinforce the cool, casual image of the script, a real-life cock-a-snook,' adds Agnello with a smile.

This was the genesis of the iconic bungee-jumping ad. It was a game-changer that would redefine the brand's image. The scene is set at a bungee-jumping point, where a group of young men and women are caught in the thrill of adventure. But when the young man at the drinks counter realizes that the stock of Thums Up has run out, the mood shifts. He's offered a different cola, but his response is unwavering—he refuses. His eyes suddenly lock on to a Thums Up truck winding its way through the treacherous valley below. In that moment, a bold idea ignites within him. Without hesitation, he makes the radical decision to bungee-jump down the mountain to seize the bottle from the truck.

What happens next leaves everyone breathless. The crowd watches in disbelief as he leaps, defying convention and fear. With perfect timing, he grabs the bottle of Thums Up from the truck and effortlessly rises back to the top, met with raucous cheers from the stunned onlookers. This wasn't just about getting a drink—it was a statement of sheer willpower. The young man displayed unmatched mental fortitude, impeccable timing and an unyielding commitment to one thing and one thing only: Thums Up. For him, there could be no compromise—it was Thums Up, or nothing.

Sales grew. By 1996, Thums Up was doing better than Coke and Pepsi.

'Before launching the ads, we used a radio-theatre format where the story and its primary postulate are read out to participants in a meditative state and they are asked to imagine the scenario,' says Agnello. This ensured that the ad connected with the emotions that Thums Up wanted to show.

Another round of consumer surveys was done, which now showed that strength need not be physical or mental but that it was more about the strength of emotion—that of a 'caring man'. The masculinity was retained but now he was an emotionally sensitive man too. It clicked with the consumers once again! Thums Up continued its upward journey. Says Priya Lobo of Ormax, 'We asked the question, "What is the smart element needed to get into the tough man image?" The scriptwriter does not know how the consumer will relate to what he has written. We did the study in small cities, like Ranchi and Gwalior, to understand how the definition of "man" was evolving in the minds of the current generation.'

With the brand's sales growing again, by 2002–03, Sharma and his team decided to take the battle head-on to the market leader, Pepsi Cola. Thums Up didn't want to remain number two to Pepsi. The research they commissioned was designed to find weaknesses in their competitor. Pepsi was selling to a younger generation, while Thums Up was for the twenty-five-plus age group. To grow the consumer base further—from the adult, out-of-home consumers—the brand began targeting teens in India with its immensely successful 'Grow Up to Thums Up Challenge' campaign.

'See, the last thing teens and young adults want to hear is that they are consuming kiddy stuff. They didn't want to be called "little boys and girls". Pepsi's strength was that it was sweeter and that it had a younger segment to be catered to. The idea was to convert both the strengths of the competition into a weakness. So the messaging was that while Pepsi Cola is a diluted, sweeter version of cola, Thums Up is for the grown-ups,' Sharma says.

By harping on the fact that Thums Up tastes 'stronger', the new campaign for the brand was meant to reposition Pepsi as a drink for kids. Coca-Cola never pitched Coke in direct confrontation with Pepsi. The company took the fight to the street with Thums Up. In an ad we see Salman Khan asking viewers if they had grown up to Thums Up. In what appears to be a college campus, Salman is seen conducting a blind test. He asks a volunteer what his favourite drink is. The reply is bleeped out, but we know what the answer is. The teenager is asked what a 'kid's drink' is. The teenager replies that it is something that is sweet. When he is asked to point out which drink has 'thunder', the student points to Thums Up. The point is emphatically made.

Thums Up won once more, hands down! Pepsi never recovered. As per a Yahoo finance report of 2023, while Thums Up has a 16 per cent market share, Coca Cola's namesake brand has a 9 per cent hold over the market. Pepsi accounts for 8 per cent of the overall carbonated soft drinks market in India.[4]

Today, the brand's scale and size dwarfs all other aerated brands in the country. Maaza, which Coke acquired from Parle along with Thums Up, contributed ₹2,826 crore in sales in 2021 and is larger than brand Coke itself in term of revenue.[5]

With its clout overshadowing every other brand, the Coca-Cola management is not leaving Thums Up on the sidelines any more. According to Sanket Ray, president for India and Southwest Asia at Coca-Cola, the company management's seriousness about the brand is reflected in its recent initiatives like placing it at the forefront of major sporting events, like the Olympic and Paralympic Games. He says:

> Our local Thums Up brand has become a billion-dollar brand in India driven by focused marketing and execution plans. We are also investing in diversity, equity and inclusion for the next wave of growth. We are extremely proud of walking the

4. Navdeep Yadav, 'Coca-Cola And Pepsi Face New Threat in India as Country's Richest Person Revives Iconic Brand', Yahoo Finance, 28 March 2023, https://finance.yahoo.com/news/coca-cola-pepsi-face-threat-114831176.html, accessed on 4 April 2025.

5. 'Maaza bigger than Coke with Rs 2,826 cr sales in FY21, Limca at Rs 2,061 cr', ET Brand Equity, 16 February 2022, https://brandequity.economictimes.indiatimes.com/news/business-of-brands/maaza-bigger-than-coke-with-rs-2826-cr-sales-in-fy21-limca-at-rs-2061-cr/89606935#:~:text=Business%20of%20 Brands-,Maaza%20 bigger%20than%20Coke%20with%20Rs%20 2%2C826%20cr%20 sales%20in,re%2Dentered%20the%20Indian%20 market, accessed on 4 April 2025.

> talk with this vision and expanding it further in terms of our product communication and partnerships as well. Our recent associations [Olympic and Paralympic Athletes for Thums Up 'Palat De' (Flip It Over) and 'Taane Palat De (Flip the Taunts)'] are a big breakthrough in this new thinking.[6]

Thums Up may have already won the toughest of its battles and has since established itself on a foundation that would be hard to destabilize. But brand and market experts believe that the $1 billion mark is just one milestone in its forty-five-year-long journey. There is still more for it to achieve.

As we see in the story of Thums Up, it is a brand which not only realized its inherent strength but also continued to evolve while addressing its target segment. From its macho image to that of mental strength and changing its communication to remain relevant has been a strong point for Thums Up. It is a classic case of the parent company quickly realizing its mistake of wanting to 'kill' the brand but then reviving it to take it to the number-one spot. Relentless focus on the product's inherent strength of being a strong cola, using consumer feedback to continuously keep the brand relevant and extensive marketing has ensured that the brand has remained number one over the past thirty years.

The billion-dollar brand continues to grow. It is a great lesson in marketing to focus on core strength while changing its communication to match the times. It is also a lesson on how to use market research to understand the core value proposition and continue to evolve.

---

6. Arnab Dutta, 'Tasting the thunder', accessed on 4 April 2025.

26

TAJ HOTELS: AN ENDURING LEGACY BUILT ON CUSTOMER SATISFACTION

There are some market segments, like essential consumer goods and high-end luxury products, where a brand can take the top spot and stay there for decades. But in some sectors, the brand has to live up to its promise every single day. Hospitality is one such sector, and the customer is often unforgiving if the services offered are not up to the mark. And there are hundreds of reasons, often beyond the control of the service provider, that may result in the customer's expectations not being met. This is what differentiates a good hotel from the others. And it is not easy to define 'good service' unless the hospitality partner has spent enormous amounts of time trying to understand what the customer really finds delightful.

Taj Hotels is synonymous with quality service in the Indian hospitality industry, and its service excellence has been built on a tremendous understanding of consumer needs and the awareness at every point in time to fulfil the 'Taj promise'.

The challenge Taj Hotels faced was to not only differentiate itself from other hotels and properties, but to continuously create a seamless customer experience which she could relate to across all its properties. It was not an easy task, but a leader must take on the most onerous responsibilities to showcase what true hospitality means. And in the capital-intensive business of hotels, which sees competition among large multinational chains, how Taj created its own unique inimitable flavour makes for a fascinating story.

Let us see how a brand leader like Taj Hotels does it.

~

'The voice of the customer is a critical part of our business,' begins Parveen Chander Kumar, executive vice president, sales and marketing at Taj Hotels, as we meet him at the plush Taj Mahal Palace in Colaba. The iconic hotel is indeed one of the finest, but we are here to hear him talk about how he delights customers every single time.

'Listening to customers and reacting is the basis of Taj's superlative experience,' Parveen says. 'And consumer insights become an essential part of the hotel industry, especially when it comes to Taj.'

Adds a manager of a Taj property: 'We take surveys, feedback and such very seriously, and we continuously act on the recommendations and suggestions given.'

Parveen elaborates:

> There are multiple channels through which the customer can leave feedback, be it on social media or in person, and we have agencies which measure Net Promoter Score. We aggressively and proactively collect customer feedback each time. It requires a lot of skill to be able to collect feedback on a daily basis, and our employees are trained to do that.

> There has been a distinct shift in our client base. Earlier, we had a large majority of foreigners but, today, a large percentage of our customers are Indians. Our communication and ad campaign reflects this trend where we talk of 'dekho apna desh' and the 'festivals of India'. We want to build nationalistic pride in Indians.

Taj, the luxury brand, is all about heritage and luxury—of creating ultra luxe, bespoke experiences for the customer, which wows them. It doesn't happen by default unless there is a conscious strategy behind it.

'We are similar to the Oberoi and the Ritz-Carlton, to name a few brands in terms of our properties—the hardware, so to say—but where we differentiate ourselves is in the warm welcome, the fond farewell, the extra mile we go, the Indian hospitality we provide,' says Parveen. He continues:

> We train our people to be intuitive to customer feedback and expectations. Most properties are similar when it comes to the 'product'—that is the rooms, the facilities, etc.—but what the customer remembers is the attention they received and the way they were treated. That is where Taj scores over all the others.

This is an insight which is easy to understand but difficult to copy. Hotels tend to focus on the hardware, while most customers remember how they were treated. This is common human behaviour. The genius of Taj was not only in recognizing this insight but in working hard, relentlessly to convert it into action.

Parveen talks of 'Taj-ness', which is the main differentiator, and is derived from a lot of consumer insights and an understanding of what will delight the customer. He says:

> Based on our continuous engagement with the customer, we have identified 200 touch points where we have an opportunity to wow the customer. If, for example, the customer is religious and we notice that she does pooja in her room, we ensure we keep fresh flowers for her when she comes back. For a smoker, we keep mints. For children, we make the room child-friendly. And for elders, we offer breakfast in the room, and so on. If our housekeeping staff finds jewellery kept on the bed, they will keep it securely in the locker and then inform the customer on how to operate the same. It is all about empowerment and creating 'magical moments', which is our mainstay for customer delight. We realize that there is only so much one can do with the product—that is, the room itself. All five-star rooms are similar, and the customer would hardly be able to differentiate between one and another. But what they will definitely remember is the way they were treated. And we customize the experience for the customer.

The process of 'culturalization', as Parveen calls it, continues even after the initial days of training. He tells us:

> We empower our people, and it pays off in a big way. For example, I had given a budget of ₹1.5 lakh to the housekeeper to use it to wow the customers. It doesn't mean he would use it for one customer but would find innovative ways to make the customer happy. For someone who has forgotten his toilet kit, he would provide a magic kit which would have all the items needed. He would provide sanitary napkins if he knows the customer may need it, and so on. We celebrate when our staff goes out of their way to help a customer. We are accommodating, unlike some of our competitors, who may offer many fancy properties but are rigid when it comes to

> what they can do for the customer. We don't throw the rule book at the customer.

This is a common experience for a traveller—the hotel being rigid about check-in and check-out timings, for instance.

'People want familiarity and a feeling of coming home. That is what they get when they come to a Taj luxury hotel,' says Parveen.

A senior executive at an MNC tells us:

> I couldn't agree more on the approach. I remember visiting a Vivanta property when I had to check in at 1.30 p.m. As the room was getting ready, I decided to have lunch on the property. Seeing me have a simple roti-and-sabzi meal, the waiter came forward and offered me a sweet dish on the house. Before that, he had offered me puchkas [Kolkata pani puri], saying, 'They may not be as great as what you get in Kolkata, but I assure you they are still pretty good. Have a plate while we prepare your meal. It is on the house.' I was surprised that the waiter had the authority to do this and had been empowered to offer me food on the house. No doubt, as a regular customer to the property, the waiter knew it was important to make me feel delighted. Such small acts go a long way in creating loyalty.

What better praise than that which comes straight from a customer's mouth!

When we tell Parveen about this, he smiles as he says, 'You are talking just about Vivanta. If you experience Taj's ultra-luxury hotels, you will be floored. The Taj Hotels brand is not about just service but also experience, and that too one which is unforgettable.'

When we ask him whether that makes Taj complacent, Parveen replies, 'We have been rated the best so many times over the past many years. But we don't rest on our accolades. Customer insights, customer understanding and making him or her delighted is a continuous process. And we don't stop at that.'

The story of Taj has been told in many ways. No one can forget how the Tata Group, led by Ratan Tata, took care of its customers during and after the infamous terrorist attack on 26 November 2008. And the way the employees and their families were treated is the stuff of HR legends.

Taj Hotels' enduring success can be attributed to several key factors, with its rich heritage and legacy being among the most prominent. Established in 1903 by Jamsetji Tata, Taj Hotels has a storied history of delivering exceptional hospitality, setting high industry standards. The brand emphasizes consistent and reliable service, ensuring guests have positive experiences at each of their properties. This commitment to excellence has earned Taj Hotels a reputation for

quality and trustworthiness.

Effective marketing strategies, including memorable advertising campaigns and celebrity endorsements, have enhanced the brand's visibility and appeal, solidifying its position in the competitive hospitality market.

Investments in training and development are central to Taj Hotels' philosophy, with a significant number of general managers being promoted from within. This approach ensures a deep understanding of the brand's ethos and fosters a culture of loyalty and expertise.

These factors, among others, have collectively ensured that Taj Hotels remains a leader in customer satisfaction and continues to uphold its esteemed position in the hospitality industry.

Brands and leaders are not built overnight. They need conviction, consistent communication, the capability to understand consumer insights and, above all, the passion of the promoter to be the leader.

CONCLUSION

To succeed in a competitive world, one has to often beat the existing leader. There is only so much space at the top. Most times, only one brand can hold a dominant position. Knowing one's enemy, or competition, is as important as knowing oneself. Changing tangible attributes are a necessary—but not sufficient—condition. Constant and correct communication is key to advertise oneself. One must make others know the attributes and qualities to 'market' oneself. And this requires relentless and consistent communication. All the elements need to be considered. As we have seen in the case studies in this section, the product, packaging, usage and the placement of the product in the house, all these were woven into the communication. A holistic approach is what ensures success. Having a good product, or a good résumé, is not enough. One must be able to communicate, market the product and let the attributes be known to those who matter.

Steve Jobs is supposed to have said, 'Design is not just what it looks like and feels like. Design is how it works.' In the early 2000s, Apple was far behind Microsoft in the personal-computer market. However, with the introduction of the iMac, iPod and, eventually, the iPhone, Apple shifted its focus from technical specs to user experience, simplicity and design. The seamless integration of hardware and software helped Apple redefine the market and become a global leader. At times, when the leader is focused on a particular segment, the new brand has a chance to become the leader by tapping into another market. Coca-Cola was the undisputed leader in beverages, but Red Bull carved out a new niche in energy drinks by targeting extreme sports and young adults. Their bold marketing campaigns, sponsorship of high-energy events and unique positioning helped them dominate the energy-drink market, while Coke remained focused on traditional sodas. Netflix adapted to digital and streaming trends, outpacing Blockbuster's outdated model. There are many more examples, but you get the point.

A deep understanding of what will 'wow' the customer is key to success. And we see that repeatedly in all the brand stories we have covered.

ABOUT THE AUTHORS

Vispy Doctor refers to himself as being 'terminally curious'. His journey has been a blend of science, business and passion. Having done his doctoral work in physics, and received an MBA degree from the Xavier School of Management (XLRI), Jamshedpur, he moved into the exciting world of branding and business consulting. Branding has always fascinated him—how small changes in perspective can have enormous consequences in the real world. But his real interests lie in astronomy, photography, spirituality and farming. These interests have kept his curiosity alive and fuelled his continuous pursuit of knowledge. Today, he spends his time between work in Mumbai and play on his farm. Life is good!

Vikrant Pande has published fourteen translations till date, many of them bestsellers, like Ranjit Desai's *Shivaji: The Great Maratha* (HarperCollins) and Girish Kuber's *Tatayan*, published as *The Tatas: How a Family Built a Business and a Nation* (HarperCollins), which won the Gaja Capital Business Book Prize for 2019. He cowrote, with Neelesh Kulkarni, *In the Footsteps of Rama: Travels with the Ramayana* (HarperCollins), a travelogue containing unknown stories of the Ramayana, which is now being made into a travel show by a top OTT producer, as well as *Akashvani: A Century of*

Stories from All India Radio (HarperCollins). He also authored *The SBI Story: Two Centuries of Banking* (Westland Publications). He is currently working on an account of fascinating operations done by the special forces (HarperCollins).

A graduate of IIM Bangalore, Vikrant Pande enjoyed twenty-five successful years in his corporate career before turning to writing full-time.

HarperCollins *Publishers* India

At HarperCollins India, we believe in telling the best stories and finding the widest readership for our books in every format possible. We started publishing in 1992; a great deal has changed since then, but what has remained constant is the passion with which our authors write their books, the love with which readers receive them, and the sheer joy and excitement that we as publishers feel in being a part of the publishing process.

Over the years, we've had the pleasure of publishing some of the finest writing from the subcontinent and around the world, including several award-winning titles and some of the biggest bestsellers in India's publishing history. But nothing has meant more to us than the fact that millions of people have read the books we published, and that somewhere, a book of ours might have made a difference.

As we look to the future, we go back to that one word—a word which has been a driving force for us all these years.

Read.